Shenanigans

Shenanigans

THE US-IRELAND
RELATIONSHIP IN
UNCERTAIN TIMES

TRINA VARGO

CAVAN
BRIDGE
PRESS

Published by Cavan Bridge Press, New York, NY
https://cavanbridgepress.com
https://www.trinavargo.com

Edited and Designed by Girl Friday Productions
www.girlfridayproductions.com
Editorial: Jane Steele
Cover Design: Paul Barrett

ISBN (Paperback): 978-0-9987493-3-4
e-ISBN: 978-0-9987493-4-1

Printed in the United States of America

*In memory of my mother and father for their
unconditional love and for teaching me
everything I know that is of any importance.*

Contents

Perhaps the best way to write is to do so as if one were already dead, afraid of no one's reactions, answerable to no one's views . . . without worrying whether you're going to offend your mother, your best friend or whether your political confreres are going to decide that you have let down the side. A writer must never let herself become a propagandist. Propagandists have a place—agitprop has a place—but I'm not that kind—I'm not that person.

—Nadine Gordimer

Introduction

It was late January 1994, and I was having difficulty falling asleep. President Bill Clinton had just granted Sinn Fein leader Gerry Adams a visa that would allow him to visit New York for forty-eight hours. The political representative of the Irish Republican Army would be restricted to travel within a twenty-five-mile radius of Manhattan. Neither my boss, Senator Ted Kennedy, nor President Clinton would meet Adams in the absence of a cease-fire by the IRA. As Kennedy's foreign policy adviser, I was sent to meet with Adams.

I was thirty-one years old and for many months had been the day-to-day negotiator for Kennedy, and effectively the White House, which refused to have any direct contact with even the New York–based publisher of the *Irish Voice*, Niall O'Dowd, who was the interlocutor for Adams and the person I spoke with several times a day. For a variety of reasons, it also served Sinn Fein to have Senator Kennedy and me in the middle. If there were disagreements, the White House version would likely be accepted over Sinn Fein's without a respected third party to keep the White House honest as well.

I was sleepless because I was anticipating my meeting with Adams that would take place the next day, February 1, at the

Waldorf Astoria, the landmark hotel in midtown Manhattan. The hotel had served as the home of the US ambassador to the UN until 2015, when a Chinese group bought the hotel and the US government feared electronic espionage. But in 1994, Ambassador Madeleine Albright resided on the forty-second floor. A little more than a year earlier, I had been one of a small group who prepared her for her confirmation hearings before the Senate Committee on Foreign Relations. But our paths would not cross at the Waldorf Astoria—the White House led on the Northern Ireland issue, and Albright was not involved.

While I appreciated what Gerry Adams was now attempting to do—bring an end to the IRA's campaign of violence—I was not an admirer. I was to serve as the counterbalance to the uncritical adulation of his supporters who would greet him on this trip, a visit that would receive blanket news coverage, including an interview on *Larry King Live*, CNN's popular prime-time television show.

The controversial Adams visit was the culmination of months of behind-the-scenes negotiations, capped by a month-long, very public disagreement between the US and UK governments. A year earlier, Clinton had been inaugurated as president of the United States. In March, he named Jean Kennedy Smith, Senator Kennedy's sister, as his ambassador to Ireland. Shortly after, Niall O'Dowd had approached me at the suggestion of Brendan Scannell, a friend of O'Dowd's who was a diplomat in the Irish embassy in Washington. If Clinton, who did not have much of a history with the issue, was to take any major initiative regarding Northern Ireland, it would not be done without the imprimatur of Ted Kennedy. Kennedy had national and international prominence and a long history on the issue going back to his first meeting with John Hume in Germany more than twenty years earlier. Hume was the leader of the Social Democratic and Labour Party (SDLP) and an advocate of peaceful change in Northern Ireland. While some on Capitol Hill were unquestioningly sympathetic to the IRA and Sinn Fein, Kennedy was not. He agreed with Hume's non-violent approach. Kennedy's support was therefore essential. If he could support a visa for Adams, it would give Clinton cover if the effort failed. As the summer of 1993 began, we were testing O'Dowd's claims that the IRA was prepared to end the violence.

O'Dowd wanted Clinton to make good on his campaign promises of appointing a special American envoy for Northern Ireland and granting a visa for Adams, commitments he had made at the urging of former congressman Bruce Morrison at a gathering in New York City in April 1992. As an adviser to the Clinton campaign on Irish issues, I was against the promise of a visa for Adams because, at that time, there was nothing going on that indicated movement toward an end to the violence and nothing to suggest that the president would keep his word. A former colleague of mine in Kennedy's office, Nancy Soderberg, who would leave Kennedy's office to go work in Little Rock on Clinton's campaign staff full-time, was less concerned. As is often the case in campaigns, promises are made to many groups on many issues because it is what they want to hear. Nancy told me she would deal with the unhappiness of broken promises after the election.

Over the course of the next year, Clinton would indeed walk back those promises. After the election, President Clinton would deny Adams a visa twice, in May and again in October 1993. He also didn't keep his promise to name a special envoy. With neither the British nor Irish governments wanting a special envoy, Clinton recognized that he couldn't unilaterally impose one.

Kennedy supported those decisions. I had been in constant conversation with O'Dowd since the spring, but even in October, the situation was not yet ripe for a visa for Adams. O'Dowd and a small group of activists were angry.

The autumn of 1993 was tense. In October, an IRA bomb exploded prematurely in a fish shop in Belfast, killing ten people, including the bomber. Retaliatory killings started immediately, and within nine days, twenty-four people were dead. Seeing Adams carry the coffin of the dead IRA bomber did not sit well with many who were contemplating an opening for Adams. There were questions about whether he could truly bring the IRA along. Despite that stomach-turning event, we focused on the positive signs.

In December, Irish taoiseach Albert Reynolds and British prime minister John Major issued their Joint Declaration on a way forward for Northern Ireland. Sinn Fein had not responded. Adams wanted talks without preconditions. Both governments demanded an IRA cease-fire prior to any talks. Kennedy visited his sister Jean Kennedy Smith in Dublin just after Christmas. Reynolds and Irish historian Tim Pat Coogan had convinced the new American ambassador that the time might be right for a visa. Senator Kennedy returned to Washington prepared to seriously consider advocating for a visa. Sensing the shift, O'Dowd had Bill Flynn, an Irish American business executive at Mutual of America, issued an invitation for Adams to speak before a foreign policy group in Manhattan. That would force the president to grant or deny a visa. While Kennedy was leaning in favor, he was not going to be bounced into anything, and he wanted to know what John Hume thought. Hume was not in Ireland when Kennedy visited, but they met in Boston in early January for the funeral of Tip O'Neill, the former Speaker of the House of Representatives. Hume gave Kennedy a green light. I'm not sure what Kennedy would have decided had John opposed the visa.

In early January 1994, once Kennedy concluded that a visa might help, battle lines were drawn. The row was heated. The British government did not want President Clinton to grant the visa, even though it had come to light in November that the British had themselves been talking with the IRA for some time. The US Departments of State and Justice were siding with the British government. Dick Canas, the president's director of counterterrorism, and someone I worked with after the 1988 bombing of Pan Am Flight 103 over Lockerbie, Scotland, was disappointed with our position, which he thought was naive. The Speaker of the House, Tom Foley, annoyed Kennedy, not because he didn't support a visa but because after telling Kennedy he wouldn't oppose it, he went behind his back to the White House to urge the president to deny the visa.

In addition to my daily conversations with O'Dowd, I stayed in touch with Sean O hUiginn in Ireland's Department of Foreign Affairs and Martin Mansergh, adviser to the taoiseach. Both were brilliant architects of the peace process. They were more visionary than the Irish ambassador to Washington, Dermot Gallagher, who was more cautious.

I was also in constant contact with Jonathan Powell, a diplomat at the British embassy who would later become Tony Blair's chief of staff. Powell had come to the US in 1991 and was then married to an American who happened to be the niece of Senator Kennedy's former press spokesperson. Despite many heated disagreements in the lead-up to the Adams visa, Jonathan and I got along and regularly made use of the British ambassador's tennis court. I had a slight edge on Jonathan in tennis, so he talked me into taking up squash, where he held the upper hand. But we were officially on opposing sides—it was my job to make sure Adams got the visa and Jonathan's to make sure he didn't. Powell was so convinced that Adams would not get the visa that we wagered lunch on the outcome. After Clinton granted the visa, Powell made good on the bet. Despite his hard work to prevent the visa, I never felt that his heart was in it—I didn't think he was personally opposed, and he would later go on to have an important role in the peace process.

Meeting Adams in my hotel room at the Waldorf Astoria was not the plan. Bill Flynn had a suite in the hotel where I was to meet Adams. But when I turned up as scheduled, not only were O'Dowd and Adams not there; some members of the press were. Spotted by one who recognized me, I was asked if I was there to meet with Adams. I ignored the question and simply said I was looking for O'Dowd and left. While we wouldn't have considered the meeting secret, it wasn't anything we announced, and I wasn't looking to be part of the story. When I got back to my room, O'Dowd called. He apologized for the confusion and suggested they come to me. It was just as well, because someone may have been listening to what went on in Flynn's suite, but it was less likely they'd bugged my room.

The hotel's heating system was not working, and my already small room was cramped even more with a couple of portable space heaters. Adams sat in the one proper armchair, O'Dowd on a small stool at the vanity table, and I sat cross-legged on the bed. It was an odd position from which to deliver my message. I told Adams that Kennedy's opposition to the IRA hadn't changed and that he believed the IRA's position had changed. We believed they were prepared to end the violence, and there should be no confusion about why this visa had been granted— Kennedy stuck his neck out and urged the president to grant it because he believed this would help Adams deliver the IRA. In a press conference later that day, Adams said he would not disappoint those who stuck their necks out for him. Our meeting was cordial. Forty minutes later, he left with a clear understanding of our views, but without his anorak. I waited until I knew he was delivering his speech in the hotel ballroom and then sought out a hotel employee who could return the coat to Adams. I obviously did not say that he'd left it in my room; there was enough scandal with the visit as it was.

In my briefing for Kennedy after the meeting, I wrote, "I found Adams surprisingly likable. He was not your stereotypical scary, raving, irrational, fanatic terrorist. He is intelligent, articulate, reasonable, had a sense a humor, and he doesn't seem to lose his temper. He was dressed in a business suit and looked like a stockbroker. . . . He seemed very relaxed and not at all hostile. He seemed very sincere when he talked about his desire to end the violence. He is either being honest or he is an incredibly good liar."

That night at the Waldorf, someone violently trying to get into my room awakened me from a deep sleep. I froze with fear, quickly assuming this visit must have something to do with the one earlier that day. After some time, the person was violently trying to get into the next door down the hall, and I concluded someone perhaps had simply had too much to drink and was trying to find their room by process of elimination.

That visa and the visit did turn out to be instrumental in the process, and seven months later, the IRA declared a cease-fire, followed soon after with a cease-fire by the Loyalist para-militaries. Four years later, Senator Mitchell ushered in the Belfast Agreement (a.k.a. the Good Friday Agreement) after exhibiting great patience as chairman of the peace talks.

Not long before the Belfast Agreement was signed, I let Senator Kennedy know that I would leave his employ after more than a decade to create a nonprofit organization that would focus on the future of the US-Ireland relationship. Those years in the mid-nineties marked the beginning of the end of a certain kind of relationship, and it would have to evolve or it would fade away. Existing Irish American organizations were not addressing this evolution, and I wanted to start an organization that would.

It was a good time to depart. The years from 1987 to 1998 were an incredible period in history, and I had been fortunate to be with Senator Kennedy as a young foreign affairs staffer on Capitol Hill during that time. In 1989, the Berlin Wall came down, and Vaclav Havel became the president of

Czechoslovakia. In 1990, Lech Walesa was elected president of Poland. That same year, Nelson Mandela was released from prison, and by April 1994, he would become the president of South Africa. At the very moment we were contemplating asking President Clinton to grant a visa for Adams, on the south lawn of the White House, Israeli prime minister Yitzhak Rabin and PLO chairman Yasser Arafat signed a Middle East peace accord. I think that most of us present on that occasion felt anything was possible.

In January 1998, I accompanied Kennedy on his first visit to Northern Ireland. While there, we visited with Mo Mowlam, the British government's secretary of state for Northern Ireland. Mo's direct and casual manner was a welcome breath of fresh air compared with that of her predecessor, Sir Patrick Mayhew, a pompous man for whom Kennedy barely concealed his contempt. I was happy to have another woman in the mix, and one who was good fun as well. There is a lot of sexism in Northern Ireland politics, and while the male Unionist politicians in particular didn't know what to make of me, Mo confused them even more. I noticed Kennedy appreciating a chess set Mo had in Hillsborough Castle—the pieces were related to Northern Ireland with one set of pawns being Royal Ulster Constabulary (RUC) members (police) and the other being IRA gunmen. I remembered it when I was trying to think of a gift to give Kennedy when I was leaving his employ. Mo's adviser, Nigel Warner, introduced me to the artist so I could purchase a set for Kennedy and one for myself. On Mo's next trip to Washington, she brought them with her, and when Kennedy was out of his office at a meeting, I set up the board so it would be there upon his return. It remained prominently displayed in his small "hideaway" office in the Capitol until his death.

"The Irish never get their act together like Jewish Americans do and Greek Americans do. What are they gonna do when I'm not around anymore?" When Kennedy said this to me in the mid-1990s, his not being around seemed implausible. He was elected to the Senate in 1962, the same year I was born. But he was adept at looking far down the road, including to a time when he wouldn't be around any longer, which would be just a decade after we had that conversation.

Kennedy's comments and my own experience spurred me to create the US-Ireland Alliance. Witnessing a rapidly changing America and Ireland, I was thinking ahead to the day when Ireland would no longer enjoy the place of prominence on the American political agenda that it did in the 1990s. While fighting to obtain the visa for Adams, I couldn't help but notice the number of Rhodes Scholars in the Clinton administration who had studied at Oxford, and I thought it would be of long-term benefit to the relationship if we could steer some of America's future leaders to study on the island of Ireland. (Ours would be called George J. Mitchell Scholars.) At the time, the Irish economy was booming, and it was clear that the large numbers of Irish emigrating to the US would continue to decline; in fact, many had returned home at the encouragement of Ireland's political leaders. After 2008, with America's own economy in the worst shape since the Depression, the Irish leaving their country followed the jobs to places like Australia and Canada. All of this means that the future of the relationship cannot simply rely on waves of immigration. Nor should we want it to—that's like hoping for, and counting on, Ireland to fail.

It was also evident that the demographics of America were changing and that Irish Americans' historical lock on political positions would diminish. For decades, Ireland relied on a handful of hugely influential politicians—House Speaker Tip O'Neill and Senate committee chairmen Ted Kennedy and Daniel Patrick Moynihan, a Democrat from New York—to sort out whatever needed to be addressed in the relationship.

In July 1998, just after creating the Alliance, I warned in a *Washington Post* opinion piece that with a wealthy Ireland

and a lessening of attention to Northern Ireland, Irish America was becoming a constituency without a cause, that complacency could lead to disintegration, and that Irish America and Ireland must develop a dynamic new relationship that is broader than the narrow ground of Northern Ireland.

Ireland was no longer a poor country in need of handouts from its rich American cousins. Between 1995 and 2007, Ireland's economy was outpacing our own. Even after the 2008 economic crash, Ireland was not a poor country. Many Irish went all in during the Celtic Tiger years, believed the hype, and flew too close to the sun. Conversely, the perpetually skeptical never developed confidence, thought it all a mirage, and then felt vindicated. Both were wrong.

The positive developments in Northern Ireland and the Irish economy were like shifting tectonic plates. This shift left the political and diplomatic establishment in Ireland and Northern Ireland issueless in US political terms. There had always been a simple ritual to the way things were done, a pattern that continued well past its sell-by date. Political leaders from the island came to Washington each St. Patrick's Day and continued to represent the Ireland of thirty years ago. The president and Congress were asked if something can be done for the Irish who are illegally in the US and for support for the outdated International Fund for Ireland. The relationship has for too long been largely about what the US can *give* to Ireland. This approach has worn thin with most American politicians and philanthropists. If Ireland and Northern Ireland don't radically and more quickly recalibrate their relationship with America, they will soon find no one is at home when they come knocking. That is already happening.

I believe that the relationship is worth maintaining. The US and Ireland share the strong bonds of history and family ties, and the US is also an important market for Irish goods and the expansion of Irish companies. Ireland serves as the home for a lot of American corporations, many chasing low corporate tax rates. It is also culturally convenient and comfortable for these companies to be in an English-speaking country, where they can access employees from the entire European Union. Additionally, there are vibrant cultural ties, and a resurgence of interest in Ireland came with the 1990s' film adaptation of Roddy Doyle's *The Commitments*, U2, and Riverdance. Irish film, music, theater, and literature remain popular with Americans. The US also serves as a pool of students who are willing to provide cash to underresourced Irish universities.

A strong relationship can exist, but it must be built on the basis of education, culture, and business, not fading nostalgia. Politics will have less prominence in the relationship, but that is a positive thing, the result of the success of those on the island and friends in the US. Ireland no longer requires America's daily attention.

When I created the US-Ireland Alliance, it was always with the very real question of whether a critical mass would recognize these subtle shifts and be interested in nurturing a different relationship. Twenty years later, I still find myself wondering if there is critical mass. Americans are now thought of as white, Latino, and black; distinctions between white Americans (Italian, Irish, etc.) have faded. Is there sufficient interest in reshaping the relationship for future generations? Do the Irish care enough to dramatically reverse the habit of being the supplicant? The jury is still out.

On September 11, 2001, I was on America West Flight 85, which took off from Washington's Reagan National Airport at 8:59 a.m., minutes after the first hijacked plane crashed into the north tower of the World Trade Center, and at about the same time the second plane hit the south tower. I was bound for Las Vegas, where, in a couple of days, singer Maura O'Connell was to perform a benefit concert for the US-Ireland Alliance. About forty minutes into the flight, unbeknownst to us, a third hijacked plane crashed into the Pentagon, just a couple of miles from where we departed. Within a half hour, the final hijacked plane would be crashed by its brave passengers, in bucolic Pennsylvania, a mere twenty miles from where my family resides. Our plane's pilot announced, "There have been major attacks on the East Coast. All planes must land immediately." Nothing similar to this had ever occurred in the US, but passengers on our plane were calm. I suspect everyone was trying to imagine what had happened and where it had happened. Having been very involved with Senator Kennedy in the aftermath of the 1988 bombing of Pan Am Flight 103, I was thinking that they never land all planes; there must be bombs on planes. I obviously didn't share this thought with my fellow passengers, but our diverted landing in Indianapolis couldn't come soon enough for me. The pilot said nothing else, which was probably best; given where our flight had originated, there would have been some chance that people on the plane knew people in the Pentagon. I recall the rest of the flight as being silent. It was not until we entered the terminal and saw the surreal images on the televisions that we learned what had happened. My flight itinerary from that day hangs next to my front door to remind me that every day could be my last. It also reminds me of what is important, that everything is relative, and I hope it emboldens me.

This book is a look, and often a hard look, based on my experiences, at the relationship between Ireland and Irish America and the things that are holding it back. The future of the relationship is uncertain, and a massive disservice is being done by failures, misunderstandings, missed opportunities, complacency, benign neglect, and even some intentional sabotage. I did not come lightly to the decision to write this book. There came a point, however, when I concluded that remaining silent made me part of the problem. Not "leaning in" would allow the people referred to in this book, and those like them, to continue with business as usual. Numerous people, most of them Irish, also urged me to write. Many have had similar experiences and feel they cannot speak up because they fear the payback that would follow.

Irish people always ask why I bother. Some who ask this question left Ireland in the 1980s. They feel like the country let them down, and they can't be bothered with it now. They profess to know all too well what I describe in this book, and many tell me it's the reason they left Ireland. The others ask this in a suspicious way—they can't make out why one would care.

I tend to be optimistic, even idealistic. One reason it has taken me so long to write this book is that I much prefer to focus on the positive and the future, and I have set this aside regularly. I also mistakenly assumed that those who felt threatened by the changing relationship would come to accept the inevitable and perhaps embrace our work. But resistance and a whispering campaign continue, and therefore must be challenged. One reason I have continued to hang in there is the inspiration I receive daily from our George J. Mitchell Scholars and the many wonderful people I work with—Irish and American. My other difficulty in writing comes from my penchant for discretion. But the problems have become pervasive. Any hope of solidifying the future of the relationship requires shining a light in some dark corners. As Astro Teller of Google X said in a TED Talk, "Enthusiastic skepticism is not the enemy of boundless optimism. It's optimism's perfect partner."

A couple of caveats: First, for the ease of the reader, I sometimes refer to Ireland, meaning the island. It gets tiresome to repeatedly use "the island of Ireland" or "Northern Ireland and Ireland" in an effort to be politically correct and precise. I trust the reader will understand what I mean. No political statement is intended.

Second, this book is a recounting of my own experiences. While I will refer to the US-Ireland Alliance—as it is from the vantage point of founding and running the organization I speak—my views are my own.

As Ireland and the US consider the future of a historic relationship, it must begin with an honest reckoning.

People desperately wish to feel "ethnic" precisely because they have all but lost the prerequisites for "being" ethnic.

—Stephen Steinberg, *The Ethnic Myth*

Chapter 1

IRISH AMERICA

What Is Irish America?

There is nothing more indicative of the nonexistent Irish American vote and diminishing political influence than a couple of St. Patrick's Day parades in 2014. Two new mayors—Marty Walsh in Boston and Bill de Blasio in New York City—refused to march because members of the LGBT community were not welcomed. The Boston Beer Company, Heineken, and even the most iconic of Irish brands, Guinness, withdrew their support for the parades. Politicians and companies were more concerned about the power and influence of the LGBT community than they were about the Irish. That's because Irish American influence has been exaggerated.

As fewer Irish have immigrated to the US in the last two decades, and as America has become more post-ethnicity (most of us are a mix of various ancestries), fewer Americans tick the box on the US census form that denotes Ireland as their ancestral home. A couple of decades ago, the number was forty-four million. That number has declined to thirty-three million, but the degree to which they identify with Ireland in any meaningful way varies widely, with the vast majority having very little connection.

Catholic Irish Americans are mainly descendants of those forced to flee Ireland during the Famine in the mid-nineteenth century. They brought with them to America an understandable hatred of the British, whom they saw as the source of their misery. In the late 1960s and early 1970s, many of the descendants of these emigrants learned of the unfair discrimination and brutal intimidation inflicted upon the Catholic minority in Northern Ireland and watched on television as British troops beat peaceful civil rights demonstrators. Steeped in anti-British animosity passed down through the generations, many believed that the solution to Northern Ireland's problems was getting the British out.

More than half of Irish Americans are Protestant. Most of their ancestors immigrated to the United States decades before the Famine and quickly assimilated. Some later began to label themselves as Scotch Irish in an effort to disassociate themselves from the recently arrived Famine Irish who were being discriminated against because of their Catholicism and poverty.

Most of today's Protestant Irish Americans have no feelings of kinship with Ireland. For those over fifty years of age, the interest in defining themselves as Irish was, to some extent, a result of the phenomenon of *Roots*. In 1977, Americans were glued to the television miniseries based on Alex Haley's book that followed the lives of generations of an African American family from the time they were brought to America as slaves. A record one hundred million people watched the final two-hour episode. *Roots* sent many Americans in search of their own ancestry. But without the opportunity to celebrate their heritage in a country that has long considered being Irish as synonymous with being Catholic, this Protestant half of Irish America remains largely invisible.

The Nonexistent Irish Vote

There is no monolithic Irish America. No cohesive entity. No voting bloc. For electoral purposes, we are simply a segment of white Americans of European descent.

In 2010, Martin O'Malley campaigned to be reelected governor of Maryland. Despite his own personal connections to, and affection for, Ireland, the great-grandson of Irish emigrants told *Irish Times* journalist Seán Flynn, "Irishness per se does not deliver a huge political dividend." That's because there is no Irish vote. If there ever was such a thing, it hasn't existed at the national level for decades. Discrimination against Catholic Americans led them to rally around the campaign of John F. Kennedy. There was talk of an Irish American vote during the Ronald Reagan and Bill Clinton elections, but that was somewhat misleading in that Catholic Americans who were Irish may have voted on the basis of their Catholicism (over issues such as abortion and the death penalty), but very few did on the basis of Irish issues. Today, Irish Americans are Democrats and Republicans, and we vote on issues like the economy, health care, immigration, education, etc. Few vote on the basis of candidates' positions on Irish issues. A large number of Irish Americans voted for Donald Trump, belying the long-held assertions of some that Irish Americans are disproportionately Democrats.

While the number of American Jews is much smaller (5.3 million) than the number of Irish Americans, a fear for the very existence of the state of Israel is a rallying factor for some American Jews. There is no issue involving Ireland that causes similar concern among a large number of Irish Americans. Another reason Jewish Americans have political and civic clout in the US is their generosity when it comes to philanthropy and political contributions. When I created the US-Ireland Alliance in 1998, the American Israel Public Affairs Committee (AIPAC) had an annual budget of $45 million. In 2014, it was more than $69 million. Despite the much larger number of Irish Americans, no Irish American organization remotely approaches that level of political influence.

In the thirty years prior to the 1998 signing of the Belfast Agreement, Irish America's identity had been largely defined in one way or another by "the Troubles" in Northern Ireland. Some Irish Americans sent money to the IRA, and a few even sent guns. Others followed the lead of John Hume, becoming advocates for peaceful change. But most never got involved, shying away from their Irish ancestry because they did not want to be associated with violence or with a convoluted conflict they did not understand.

For many Irish American organizations, influencing US policy on Northern Ireland had been their raison d'être. As the worst of Northern Ireland's problems were on the road to resolution in 1998, these groups largely became organizations without a cause. While most people on the island moved forward with the signing of the Belfast Agreement and the newfound economic wealth of the 1990s' Celtic Tiger, Irish Americans who most actively identified with their Irishness continued to live in the past, seemingly not wanting Ireland to come out from under their shadow.

Stella O'Leary, a minor Democratic fund-raiser in Washington, DC, and founder of Irish American Democrats; Niall O'Dowd; and New York City attorney Brian O'Dwyer regularly made claims about an Irish American vote and Irish

American political clout and donations that don't withstand scrutiny.

In April 2007, O'Leary told *Irish Times* journalist Denis Staunton that she estimated that 90 percent of Irish American Democrats backed Hillary Clinton and that 20 percent of what Hillary would raise would be "Irish money." O'Leary provided no evidence for her claims. Even a cursory look at the surnames of the contributors to Obama's campaign showed that statement to be false. O'Leary confused her small circle with Irish America writ large.

In the summer of 2009, journalist Niall Stanage wrote an *Irish Times* piece that deflated the exaggerations about Irish America's political power. O'Leary had written about the elections of Democrats Joe Crowley and Martin O'Malley, claiming that they both "rely on the Irish vote to provide a winning margin." But in running for the office of mayor of Baltimore in 1999, O'Malley won more than 90 percent of the vote and in 2004, more than 87 percent of the vote. In 2006, he won nearly 53 percent of the vote when he first ran for governor. Crowley too had won convincingly. In 2004, 2006, and 2008, he received at least 80 percent of the vote. As Stanage correctly noted, it is absurd to suggest that Irish Americans provided any "winning margin."

In 2015, O'Leary spoke at the Clinton Institute for American Studies at University College Dublin. The format was a conversation with former *Irish Times* journalist Conor O'Clery. O'Clery questioned whether there was an Irish vote and said that when he was on the campaign trail with Bill Clinton when he ran for president, and with Ted Kennedy on his last Senate campaign, he "never heard Ireland raised once."

O'Leary again claimed that Crowley's election was evidence of the power of the Irish vote. She said his district is "18 percent Irish. His vote is 45 percent Irish because the others are not voting (Indians, Afghanis)." But US Census figures show that Irish Americans made up only 3.7 percent of Crowley's district.

About 47 percent of Crowley's district was Latino, 25 percent white, 16 percent Asian, and 10 percent African American. The 2016 edition of the *American Almanac of Politics* includes information on Crowley's 2014 Congressional race. He received 88 percent of the vote (50,352 votes). The total population of the district is around 700,000 people. If you subtract the approximate 25 percent of the population under the voting age, that means only about 10 percent of those of voting age in the district actually voted.

The *2011 Fast Facts Census* breaks down "white" into twenty ethnic categories, with Italians being the largest, nearly double the number of Irish. The almanac said the Irish numbered 28,209.

If we assume 25 percent of the Irish were under age eighteen, that means that 21,157 is the maximum number of Irish voters. O'Leary claimed that 45 percent of Crowley's vote is Irish. In 2014, he would have had to receive more Irish votes than there are voters to hit 45 percent! The only way that could even be close would be if every single Irish person of voting age voted, and voted for Crowley, and no other white person did.

In June 2018, Alexandria Ocasio-Cortez soundly defeated Crowley in the Democratic primary. At twenty-eight years old, Ocasio-Cortez is young, Puerto Rican, socialist, and female, and she won with 57.5 percent of the vote, despite Crowley outspending her ten to one. The district is now 54 percent Latino, 26 percent African American, and 5 percent Asian. There was not, nor is there, an Irish vote.

O'Leary also claimed that "thousands of Irish Americans in 50 states who have contributed millions of dollars through Irish American Democrats' Political Action Committee over the past 13 years consciously think of themselves as Irish."

But Stanage pointed to the related election cycle records (2007–2008): "Obama raised $778,642,047 and John McCain raised $399,826,076 for their respective presidential campaigns. The FEC records indicate that during that cycle, O'Leary's Irish American Democrats raised only $35,840. Of this total, $10,840 came from individual contributors and $20,000 from other committee contributions. The FEC does not publish the names of individuals who donate less than $200. However, its records do show that of the $10,840 raised from individuals, $8,550—almost 80 percent—came from six individuals." Stanage concluded, "This brings some perspective to Ms. O'Leary's portrayal of her organization as a fundraising behemoth." Irish American Democrats thus gave Obama .0046 percent of his war chest. Irish Americans were donating to Obama, and all candidates for that matter; they just weren't giving *as* Irish Americans.

A quick look at Open Secrets, a nonpartisan organization that follows the money in US politics, shows how little O'Leary's PAC raises and doles out. The most ever raised in a cycle was $116,000 many years ago. In the two-year 2012 election cycle, the PAC gave $8,400 to fourteen candidates. In the 2014 cycle, it doled out less than $12,000, with almost half of it going to one person, Brendan Boyle, who was running for Congress in Pennsylvania. In US election fund-raising terms, this is insignificant. In the 2016 election cycle, Open Secrets reports that Irish American Democrats raised less than $50,000.

Given her own reports to the FEC, it's unclear as to how O'Leary is claiming to have raised *millions* through Irish American Democrats. Despite the low numbers, after the 2010 election, O'Leary widely distributed an email in which she claimed credit for nearly every race in the country won by a Democrat with an Irish American last name. That can only be described as delusional.

O'Bama

From 1988 through 2008, I served as Irish issues adviser for every Democratic US presidential nominee from Michael Dukakis through Barack Obama. I became involved in the Obama campaign at an early stage, when few believed he would become the nominee. In the mid-1990s, Tony Lake and I had worked together on the Northern Ireland peace process when Tony was President Clinton's national security adviser. In late 2006, Tony was advising the Obama campaign and asked if I would handle Irish issues. My decision had nothing to do with being *against* Hillary Clinton. I had a positive opinion of Obama; someone I respected asked for my advice, and I was happy to give it.

I also liked the general lack of drama about the Obama team. Such was not the case with many around Clinton. I had worked with Kris Balderston, a member of the Clinton campaign, when he was on Hillary's staff in the Senate. One day, we were talking on the phone, and something Kris said caused me to think that he was unaware that I was helping the Obama campaign. (Given that the US-Ireland Alliance is nonpartisan, I helped the campaign as a volunteer in a personal capacity but declined to be a public surrogate). When I told Kris that I was helping Obama, he paused (I sensed surprise) and then spewed that I didn't *have* to help the Clinton campaign because, technically, I had not worked for either of the Clintons. But he went on to tell me that there was a "special place in hell" reserved for those who worked for Bill Clinton and were not supporting Hillary. He specifically mentioned Tony Lake and Greg Craig, a former colleague of mine in Kennedy's office who was a senior foreign policy adviser on the Obama campaign. I was taken aback by the venom and also by the expectation that these individuals were somehow beholden to support Hillary. These were successful professionals in their own right, and while they were no doubt grateful to President Clinton for the roles he gave them in his administration, to think that meant they were something akin to indentured servants for the rest of their careers was a ridiculous notion. Years later, in the 2014 book *HRC* by Jonathan Allen and Amie Parnes, Balderston's name would surface as a keeper of the Clintons' "enemies list," a list I would not be surprised to find myself on.

In March 2007, Ancestry.com reported that Senator Obama had ancestral roots in Ireland. Two months later, on my way from Dublin to Limerick, I stopped in Moneygall to take some photos for the candidate and campaign staff. At a newsagent's shop, when I asked if anyone could tell me how to find the church associated with Obama, I was asked, "Who's Obama?" While they understandably did not know the Democratic candidate back then, they did know where the Templeharry Church was. Just a few miles away, the church was where his ancestors were reportedly baptized and where they worshipped. When I finally found the church, after initially missing the turn on the winding country roads, it was locked. A nearby farmer opened the church, told me to take my time, and showed me where to leave the key when I left.

When I wrote candidate Obama's statement on Irish issues, it included a commitment to visit Ireland if he was elected. I cleared that with those close to him, as I hate when candidates just say what people want to hear, rather than what they actually intend to do if elected. I was assured that if Obama won, he would visit. In 2011, when President Obama visited Ireland, there were suggestions that he was making the trip as part of his 2012 reelection campaign. The *Irish Independent* reported that "his popularity is likely to soar among the Irish American vote." The *Irish Examiner* claimed that the Irish American vote "will be vital" in the election. Joe Higgins, a member of the Irish Parliament, said that the security afforded the Obama visit amounted to a campaign contribution for Obama, whose visit, he claimed, was all about his reelection campaign and the Irish American vote. But the proverbial white guy in rural Pennsylvania (a place I know something about, as I come from there) made up his mind about Obama because of the economy, Social Security, health care, guns, abortion, education, Afghanistan, and several other factors, which might even include race. They were not voting for the president on the basis of his stopping in Ireland for less than twenty-four hours.

I was delighted that President Obama visited for the simple reason that there is no surer way to get a positive feeling about Ireland than to visit. We see it every year with the welcome the people of Ireland give the Mitchell Scholars. And I recall when President Clinton rang Senator Kennedy from Ireland in 1995 to say his days there were the best of his presidency. But it is silly to suggest an Irish American vote that doesn't exist. The visit simply was what it was. The president had by then already visited ten European countries, some more than once. It would have been odd if he *hadn't* visited Ireland.

A couple of months after the visit, Rosita Boland of the *Irish Times* reported on American travel writers visiting Ireland. She noted that not only did none of the journalists believe Obama's visit would have any impact on the number of tourists coming from America; they laughed at the very suggestion of it. They were correct that most Americans would not have even registered that Obama had been there. Do Irish people vote for their politicians because they've visited the US or because of their views on the US?

One thing I wondered about, and still do, was Obama's feelings about being part Irish American. While he rolls with it politically, it's hard to imagine he identifies. And why would he? Nigerian-born Chimamanda Ngozi Adichie wrote to non-American blacks in her 2013 book, *Americanah*, "When you make the choice to come to America, you become black. Stop arguing. Stop saying I'm Jamaican or I'm Ghanaian.

America doesn't care." This is not dissimilar—Obama may be part Irish American, but in the eyes of most Americans, he is simply black.

Before Obama ran for the presidency and before his Irish ancestry was revealed, I was trying to make the Illinois senator Irish. In October 2005, U2 stopped in Washington, DC, on its Vertigo tour. Band manager Paul McGuinness was on the US-Ireland Alliance advisory board and offered me tickets and backstage passes. My guest was Sharon Waxman, who replaced me as Senator Kennedy's foreign policy adviser. We were backstage after the concert, talking with Senator Obama's foreign policy staffer, Mark Lippert. We suggested to Lippert that O-bama had to be Irish, and we joked that he should insert an apostrophe.

Obama would later use his Irish ancestry in a light and joking manner, which was the right touch. Going overboard on that front would have been crassly political and inauthentic. It was a line he had to walk carefully, and he did.

But what did he think deep down about it all? Could he come from Chicago, which for years had been politically controlled by Irish Americans, and not have some resentment because he had to work harder to rise through the ranks?

In their 2012 book, *The Obamas*, Michael Powell and Jodi Kantor wrote that Michelle Obama's former colleagues said that she "particularly resented the way power in Illinois was locked up generation after generation by a small group of families, many of them white Irish Catholic." If that was her view, can you blame her?

In a 2008 piece for the *New York Times*, Powell and Kantor wrote that when Michelle Obama arrived as a student at Princeton in 1981, the mother of Catherine Donnelly, her roommate, "spent months pleading with Princeton officials to give her daughter a white roommate instead." When I read the Irish surname, I cringed and couldn't help but believe that these kinds of experiences would understandably taint the Obamas' views of Irish Americans.

During the 2008 campaign, Mulligan's Bar and Grill in Marietta, Georgia, was selling tee shirts that had the cartoon monkey from the children's books *Curious George* with Obama's image underneath. I cringed again at the Irish pub name and hoped the Obamas hadn't seen that.

While not the case with Barack Obama, many African Americans' Irish surnames come from a white slave owner. I never expect African Americans to celebrate such a connection. It is understandably too much to hope that many will take the perspective of the late, great Maya Angelou. In *African American Lives*, Skip Gates's PBS series, the Harvard professor asked Angelou if it bothered her that her great-grandfather was a white man, a slave owner. Her response: "What's to bother, it's me . . . should be pleased at whoever your ancestors were, I mean you're here." She seemed to wear lightly that which is so heavy. She added: "Heritage is so complex that we have to be simple. We have to consider ourselves global. Takes a lot of courage to do that. But human beings are more alike than we are unalike."

Racism is still very much alive, including with too many Irish Americans who forget that their ancestors were also discriminated against. As is often the case, the oppressed become the oppressors (see Noel Ignatiev's 1995 book, *How the Irish Became White*). Slaves were emancipated less than two decades after the Irish fleeing the Famine arrived in America. The Irish feared that freed slaves would take their jobs but also welcomed the fact that the Irish were no longer the lowest on the totem pole of class. A century later, many Irish Americans were less than thrilled with the Kennedy family's support for civil rights. During the 2008 campaign, after Hillary Clinton was out of the race, many Irish American political leaders were unusually slow to coalesce behind Obama. Looking at it from the vantage point of having worked with several previous campaigns, I was uneasy with that slowness and felt some of it was related to Obama's race.

At the 2008 Denver, Colorado, and 2012 Charlotte, North Carolina, Democratic conventions, the shameless attempt of Stella O'Leary's Irish American Democrats to somehow unite Obama's Kenyan and Irish ancestries fell flat. In 2012, O'Leary and Brian O'Dwyer were promoting McBlackPAC (no kidding), an organization that reportedly was to lobby for the shared interests of both Irish Americans and African Americans. If you're scratching your head, so was everyone else.

It is surprising how this sort of thing gets reported as serious news in Ireland. In the *Irish Times* on September 5, 2012, Lara Marlowe wrote that McBlackPAC "was seeking to correct the under-representation of blacks in public office." In fact, it was just another O'Leary/O'Dwyer overreach to suggest relevancy.

Unchallenged was O'Leary's claim that "the Irish who took the soup moved to the Republican Party once they made some money. . . ." "Took the soup" is a reference to Irish Catholics who, during the Famine, would be fed by the Protestant church if they converted. Ergo, they were fed in Ireland and didn't have to emigrate. O'Leary's comment makes no sense by any stretch of the imagination.

According to Open Secrets, McBlackPAC never raised or spent a penny.

Thankfully, Irish Americans are no longer a group discriminated against. By 2008, the time had come to recognize and embrace the fact that Irish America was now part of the US political mainstream. But some have been slow to give up their sense of victimhood.

Those who falsely suggest an Irish vote will often state that x percent of Irish Americans voted for y candidate. But except for the Latino vote, pollsters don't break down voting on the basis of ethnicity. What some claim as an Irish American vote is actually the Catholic vote, though the Catholic vote is not an accurate reflection of an Irish vote. For starters, more than half of Irish America is Protestant, so more than half of Irish America is left out of this equation. There is also the fact that the Irish are but one piece of the Catholic vote. Latinos now make up the largest segment of it, which also includes Italians, French, Poles, etc. Nor can you assume that all Irish American Catholics vote the same way. And the Catholic vote sways not only between candidates but between parties. It is inaccurate and misleading to suggest the Catholic vote is synonymous with an Irish vote.

Catholic voters are of interest to pollsters because they are swing voters—they have been on the winning side of presidential elections since 1972. In 2008, Hillary Clinton got the majority of the Catholic vote in the Democratic primaries, but she didn't win the nomination. If you believe there is an Irish vote and that Hillary Clinton got it, that would mean that Obama won *despite* it. (Trump won the Catholic vote in 2016.)

Demographics and political power have been rapidly changing in America. In 2011, Rahm Emanuel became the first Jewish mayor of Chicago, a city long led by the Daleys. When Thomas Menino became the mayor of Boston in 1993, he was the first non-Irish mayor in sixty years. Ted Kennedy, Tip O'Neill, and Daniel Patrick Moynihan are all dead, and most members of Congress who have Irish ancestry don't identify with the country to the extent previous generations did.

Some Irish will also go along with the fiction of Irish American influence because, as a prominent Irish journalist once told me, "It's what we want to believe about ourselves." But these misrepresentations result in complacency about the real work that needs to be done to secure the relationship for future generations.

Tough Love

The Irish need to be honest with themselves, with one another, and they should also expect nothing less from America.

Friends of Ireland, including US politicians, should speak honestly with the Irish. Congressman Richie Neal, a Massachusetts Democrat in the US House of Representatives, was a guest on a popular evening news program on Irish television when Ireland was negotiating with the IMF after the economic crash of 2008. The interviewer asked Neal if he and other prominent Irish American politicians weren't, quietly, behind the scenes, trying to negotiate a better deal for Ireland with the IMF. He was also asked if he would be steering American companies to set up in Ireland. Neal never directly answered the questions, I assume because he was being polite. But we do a disservice by not being frank in the way that true friends are. He should have honestly said that, no, Irish American politicians were not secretly negotiating with the IMF, and if he encouraged US companies to set up in Ireland, when unemployment was high at home, his constituents would vote him out of office.

In November 2007, I wrote an opinion piece in the *Irish Times* in which I merely stated the obvious, that if US immigration reform comes, it will be—and should be—comprehensive, but there would not be a "special deal" for Irish immigrants illegally in the US. My honesty resulted in a torrent of attacks by Niall O'Dowd, the same O'Dowd I'd worked with on the peace process and who had been a member of the advisory board of the US-Ireland Alliance for several years. As a friendly Irish journalist told me in response to O'Dowd attacking me, "Everything you wrote was completely true, you just shouldn't have said it." As long as that mind-set continues, and as long as people—Irish and Irish American—are attacked for speaking truth to power, the US and Ireland will not truly enjoy a mature relationship.

What has been traditionally seen as Irish America is a stereotype that most people in Ireland don't relate to, nor do most Irish Americans. Many of those most engaged in ethnic politics are frequently out of touch with the countries to which they feel so attached, as well as with most Americans who share the same ancestry. While they are often the loudest, they are not the most representative and often advocate positions that can be at odds with sound American foreign policy as well as the views or needs of the countries in question. They are often, as the saying goes, "more Irish than the Irish."

Some Irish Americans have long been out of step with the Irish in Ireland, and the Irish are often perplexed. In an interview with the *Boston Globe* in April 2011, Diarmuid Martin, the archbishop of Dublin, when asked about his ties to the US, said that he had "no feeling for Irish-Americanism. I don't understand it. . . . American sentimentalism for a country they don't know, it's not my dish." The interviewer was asking about Cardinal Sean O'Malley, an Irish American from Boston whom the pope had selected to assist Ireland with the handling of the clergy-abuse crisis. When asked if it mattered that O'Malley's ancestors came from Ireland, Martin said no: "in fact, coming to Ireland and playing the Irish-American card can actually be—today, there would be a certain amount of skepticism. He's an American churchman, I'm an Irish churchman. . . . What we have in common is not our Irishness, it's our Catholicity."

A small but vocal group of Irish Americans has been more conservative than the Irish themselves. Some of the Irish American organizations that rightly demanded an "inclusive" Northern Ireland, with equality for Catholics, have themselves long practiced the politics of exclusion—the exclusion of Protestants, women, minorities, and the LGBT community. In April 2008, after *Sunday Tribune* journalist Marion McKeone attended a New York Irish event, she summed it up: "It's a curious thing, that a group that so assiduously . . . and deservedly . . . claims credit for its role in ushering in a new era in Northern Ireland clings so tightly to the trappings of the oppressed."

The US-Ireland Alliance

I created the US-Ireland Alliance in 1998 to address a changing US-Ireland relationship. For decades, Ireland had been a poor country to which the US sent remittances. The boom in the Irish economy that began in the mid-1990s changed all that. The relationship had also been heavily about the Troubles— the Belfast Agreement in 1998 resulted in a decreased political interest from the US. Immigration was a significant issue in the 1980s, but, with fewer Irish moving to the US beginning in the 1990s, the relationship is also less about that. The US-Ireland Alliance is focused on educating Americans about modern Ireland and building a contemporary relationship that is more partnership than paternalistic.

Our different activities are referenced throughout this book. Our flagship project is the George J. Mitchell Scholarship program. Every year, about three hundred people across the US compete for one of twelve scholarships for a year of postgraduate study in Ireland. The recipients must appear to be future leaders in their fields, and in addition to academic excellence, they must have records of leadership and service to others. The program is now one of the most prestigious scholarships in the US. Over the years, the majority of individuals lucky enough to be offered interviews for both the Mitchell and the Rhodes (to study at Oxford) have opted for the Mitchell. There are now more than two hundred Mitchell Scholars, and their connection to Ireland is part of building a relationship for future generations.

The US-Ireland Alliance also holds an annual event in Hollywood that honors the Irish in the arts, particularly in film. Excellence in the arts is perhaps one of Ireland's two best contributions to the world, the other being the people they've shared with so many countries. The event has resulted in many collaborations and allowed several Irish artists to achieve greater recognition in the US. For the last number of years, we've held the event at director J.J. Abrams's Bad Robot production company. This association was the genesis of J.J.'s interest in Ireland, and that would lead to his filming part of *Star Wars: The Force Awakens* on Skellig Michael off the western coast of Ireland. The tourism value to the Irish economy of that film, and that of *The Last Jedi*, is incalculable.

We are also creating materials so that high school teachers in the US may teach their students about Ireland, and we have held golf tournaments in Ireland to introduce Irish and American business leaders. Through these various strands, we aim to educate several demographics about Ireland and have a positive impact on the relationship.

The American Ireland Fund—The First Order of Business Is Always the Split

When I was creating the US-Ireland Alliance, I reached out to the American Ireland Fund. I assumed that they would see the Alliance as complementary. I was wrong.

Irishman Tony O'Reilly and Dan Rooney, the owner of the Pittsburgh Steelers, created the American Ireland Fund in 1976, when Ireland was a poor country and the organization was a vehicle by which wealthy Irish Americans could send contributions to Ireland. That was a worthy and successful endeavor. By the time I created the Alliance in 1998, Ireland was a very wealthy country; not only did most in my generation not feel a need to send remittances to Ireland, but I was constantly meeting Irish people who did not like what they viewed as the American Ireland Fund's paternalistic approach.

The AIF's mission had become outdated. I believed that what was necessary for the future was to educate Americans about contemporary Ireland, create a peer-to-peer relationship, and engage a new generation—and not just Irish Americans, but a diverse cross section of Americans. I thought and hoped that the AIF might understand my focus, and perhaps even support it.

When word was getting out in early 1998 that I was leaving Kennedy's office to start a new organization, Paul Quinn, a Washington, DC, lobbyist and AIF member, contacted me to ask if I would instead come work for the American Ireland Fund. I politely declined because I was interested in a different direction for the relationship. Unhappy with my answer, Quinn contacted Senator Kennedy's chief of staff to suggest that the senator convince me to work for the American Ireland Fund. Kennedy supported my plans and declined to try to talk me out of them.

At the helm of the AIF were Loretta Brennan Glucksman and Kingsley Aikens. Glucksman was the wife of Lou Glucksman, the wealthy Wall Street trader who featured in Ken Auletta's book, *Greed and Glory on Wall Street*. Loretta was thus able to be philanthropic and became the chair of the AIF. Aikens was the CEO.

Hoping that we might work together, or at least not be at odds, I went to Manhattan to meet with Loretta at a restaurant near New York University. We had a pleasant lunch, and she appeared to understand my objectives and personally support them. She was so enthusiastic that I thought she might write a check on the spot, even though I hadn't met her to ask for money. At the end of the lunch, she said that all she had to do was "talk to Tony," referring to Tony O'Reilly, the CEO of H. J.

Heinz, who had built the American Ireland Fund and was still the power behind it.

After that lunch, I never heard from Loretta again. I tried following up several times and received no response. Given her personal, positive reaction at lunch, it seemed that someone had dissuaded her. Soon after, I was told by some within the American Ireland Fund that they felt my plans for the US-Ireland Alliance could draw donations away from them, and the word went out that the US-Ireland Alliance was not to be supported. Brian Burns, a San Francisco–based AIF supporter who had previously committed to giving our new organization $10,000, reneged. Over the years, when I would inevitably bump into Loretta at various events, she would look at me a bit sheepishly—she knew that I knew she thought the Alliance was a great idea.

There was a brief period in 2001 when I mistakenly thought that perhaps those with the American Ireland Fund had reconsidered and might wish to work together. Following the terrorist attacks on September 11, 2001, several of our Irish supporters said that they would like to do something. We came up with the idea of raising funds to offer a trip to Ireland to the families of the firefighters and police officers who lost their lives that day while trying to rescue others. We called it the Innisfree project after the Yeats poem because a line in the poem was evocative of the respite we hoped Ireland would provide: "And I shall have some peace there, for peace comes dropping slow."

I pitched the idea to Taoiseach Bertie Ahern, who loved it. My biggest concern was making this offer and then not raising sufficient funds to pay for it. The Irish prime minister understood and committed the Irish government to making up the difference if we were unable to raise the funds. We raised the money, most of it from members of the Garda in Ireland and the Police Service of Northern Ireland, and we never had to take the taoiseach up on his generous offer.

When the taoiseach visited Manhattan in 2001, he announced the project in the presence of New York City mayor Rudy Giuliani. This was the first time that people outside our organization were learning of our plans. In the end, more than one hundred families took us up on the trip, and I know of at least one family that used the occasion to scatter its loved one's ashes in Ireland. Many people and organizations, including firefighters on the island, Tourism Ireland, the Irish Hotels Federation and the Northern Ireland Hotels Federation, the Car Rental Council of Ireland, and the Golf Tour Operators Association, helped make this a success. Specialized Travel Services of New York handled logistics. Aer Lingus gave a reduced price on flights. Irish barrister Bill Shipsey and solicitor Philip Lee ran a fund-raiser that involved climbing Ireland's highest peaks (Mitchell Scholars Dawn Hewett and Laela Sturdy were part of the climb). Mitchell Scholar Desha Girod helped me liaise with the many families involved.

At the beginning of this campaign, someone from the American Ireland Fund contacted me and asked me to submit an application for funding for Innisfree. I was told that the AIF wanted to do something post 9/11, didn't have a project of its own, and wanted to support Innisfree. I welcomed that as a sign that maybe the AIF's attitude toward the Alliance was softening, and we applied for the funding. I was never contacted about this again—not even to be told they had decided against funding. Later, a friendly source told me, "They just wanted to see what you were up to."

That says more about the American Ireland Fund than the US-Ireland Alliance and proves the old adage that, with the Irish, the split is always the first order of business. The Irish writer/director Neil Jordan once mentioned "spite wall" to me, a term I hadn't heard before. This is the behavioral equivalent.

Years later, after I wrote a piece in the *Irish Times* that said Ireland didn't need handouts from Americans, Kingsley Aikens, CEO of the Ireland Funds, went out of his way to approach me at a Northern Ireland Bureau reception in Washington, DC, to say, "You may be right about what you write, but they still keep writing me checks." He was grinning like a Cheshire cat when he said this.

Even after Glucksman and Aikens no longer ran the AIF, the policy of not supporting the US-Ireland Alliance and the George J. Mitchell Scholarship program continued.

In 2016, the American Ireland Fund made its first ever donation to the Mitchell Scholarship program, only after the repeated insistence of a couple of people who stood up against our being blackballed. I wish I could say I believe that this indicates a sincere change of thinking in the AIF, but there is no evidence of that.

Triage—What Ireland Can Do about Irish America

What does Ireland need to do? In a word, triage. Sorting the victims in order to increase the number of survivors is not the kind of thing the Irish like to do. It requires making hard choices, thinking of the relationship like a business. There are often obvious decisions, but slowness in implementing can be fatal.

Ireland needs to be deliberate about its relationship with the US. There needs to be a plan. Ireland needs to look at who is delivering for the relationship and invest in those people and organizations.

Ireland shouldn't settle for the Irish America it knows; it should help create the Irish America it wants. Our joint challenge is to engage many more Irish Americans and non-Irish Americans who could be interested in contemporary Ireland.

Business, education, culture, and entertainment are the paths to engaging them.

It must be asked if the Irish are sufficiently interested and invested in the relationship and will contribute to it. A 2010 report by McKinsey & Company, "Philanthropy in the Republic of Ireland," found giving by private individuals and corporations in Ireland to be very low. Ireland is not a developing country, but the confidence necessary for philanthropy has often lagged behind reality, even when the Celtic Tiger roared loudly.

Northern Ireland's years of bloodshed have thankfully ended. Since the mid-1990s, Irish immigration to the US has declined dramatically. Despite Ireland's more recent financial difficulties, the days when many Irish Americans were willing to send remittances are over. The US-Ireland relationship must be radically altered to reflect reality. In a demographically changed America, a new generation—Irish and non-Irish—must be fostered to retain the links. And vestiges of the past, which only serve as a drag on needed progress, should be jettisoned.

In 2016, there were hints of incremental change, but change seems to occur only when backs are against the wall. The Friendly Sons of St. Patrick made Anne Anderson, the first female Irish ambassador to the US, an "honorary" member. On the one hand, finally. On the other hand, seriously, "honorary"? It was the first year LGBT groups were allowed in the St. Patrick's Day parades in the US. Again, it's hard to get overly excited—Ireland passed a marriage equality referendum before LGBT groups could march in these parades.

In 2018, I urged the Irish Taoiseach to stop sending diplomats to male-only organization events in the US. It was disappointing to read Leo Varadkar's response to me in the *Irish Times*: "I don't think we could or should apply a double standard by boycotting male-only Catholic events in the US while still attending male-only events in the Vatican or the Muslim world or even gender-specific events organised by LGBT groups or women's rights groups."

I think Yeats might say that change comes dropping slow when it comes to the relationship.

Political intrigue is not really politics, and, although you can get away with superficial politics for a time, it does not bring much hope of lasting success. . . . I am happy to leave political intrigue to others; I will not compete with them, certainly not by using their weapons.

—Vaclav Havel, *Summer Meditations*

It ought to be remembered that there is nothing more difficult to take in hand, more perilous to conduct, or more uncertain in its success, than to take the lead in the introduction of a new order of things. Because the innovator has for enemies all those who have done well under the old conditions, and lukewarm defenders in those who may do well under the new.

—Machiavelli, *The Prince*

Chapter 2

THE 2008 PRESIDENTIAL CAMPAIGN

The Clintons' Enemies List

When Bill Clinton ran for president in 1992, I was the Irish issues adviser to his campaign, working with former colleague Nancy Soderberg who had left Senator Kennedy's employ to go to Little Rock, Arkansas, to work on the campaign full-time. And I worked with the Clinton White House team, which included Tony Lake and Jane Holl, throughout the peace process. But I would later end up in the Clintons' bad books, and my card was probably first marked in the fall of 2000.

It was early days for the US-Ireland Alliance, and Paul Reichler, a partner in the Foley Hoag law firm, kindly gave me use of an empty office in their Washington, DC, location, half a block from the White House. I knew Paul from when we worked together to bring free and fair elections to the South American country of Guyana years earlier. In November 2000,

Bill Clinton was president, Hillary had been elected as a senator for New York, and the first class of our George J. Mitchell Scholars had recently arrived in Ireland. I was in my office when I received a call from Senator Mitchell, telling me that the president had called him.

Seeing the network of Rhodes Scholars during the Clinton administration, and having valued my time as a Rotary Scholar in Montreal, I wanted to create a scholarship that would attract America's future leaders and send them to universities on the island of Ireland for a year of graduate study. I agreed with Senator Kennedy that there was nothing inherently partisan about Irish issues and so created a nonpartisan organization. I also knew, and Kennedy understood, that naming the scholarship after him would have closed many doors with US Republicans. While George Mitchell was a Democrat, he was not *as* polarizing a figure, and his role as chairman of the Northern Ireland peace talks lifted him above politics when it came to Ireland.

After Mitchell brokered the Good Friday Agreement, I visited him in his Washington, DC, law firm office. We knew each other slightly from Capitol Hill, but while he was chairing the peace talks, Kennedy deliberatively gave him a wide berth because he felt that if Mitchell were seen to be too close, it would compromise him when he needed to be, and be seen to be, an independent broker.

I explained to Senator Mitchell my desire to create a scholarship and asked for his permission to name it after him. He kindly agreed. Over the years, he has met nearly every class of Scholars and has taken pride in the positive difference Mitchell Scholars are already making. But he is not involved in the management of the Alliance or the Mitchell Scholarship program and has never been involved in the selection of the Scholars.

So, it was with some uneasiness that he rang me to say that President Clinton had just been onto him and that he was very unhappy that the boyfriend of his daughter, Chelsea, was not among the twenty finalists for a Mitchell Scholarship. Mitchell made clear that he was not asking me to do anything; he just wanted to understand the background and asked what he should say to the president.

In only the second year of the scholarship program, we received around two hundred applications for the twelve scholarships. (Today we receive more than three hundred.) An applicant had only a 6 percent chance of receiving one. Our then director of the scholarship program, Dell Pendergrast, and I read every application for the purpose of eliminating those applicants who had no realistic chance of winning. But we were conservative on that front, and if there was any reasonable chance, the application was forwarded to the next round, where a larger group independently read and reviewed the applications and made their recommendations as to which twenty people should be chosen as the finalists. Those twenty came to Washington, DC, in late November for an interview before a selection committee of individuals who were accomplished in their professional fields.

It would have been hard not to notice an application that included a reference letter from the sitting president of the United States. References from well-known people can cut both ways. A very good reference from someone who knows the applicant well is much better than a reference from someone famous when it is obvious that the famous person doesn't know the applicant that well. In this case, however, it was clear that the president wrote the reference and that he knew the young man well and thought highly of him. When I read the application, I thought he certainly merited passing on to the readers, but because I had read the other 199 applications, my gut told me that he was unlikely to end up as a finalist.

Dell, who previously served as a high-ranking official in the US Information Agency, thought the same. When the readers' rankings were later submitted to us, Chelsea's boyfriend had not been selected for a final interview.

Candidates in the process know that if they are chosen for a final interview, they will be contacted by a certain date. The president called Senator Mitchell before the final interviews but after it was clear that the young man had not been selected. It would be hard to believe that the timing of the president's call wasn't aimed at influencing us to make him a finalist.

Some have since told me that we are too principled, and we should have just given the young man a finalist spot—and some would say even the scholarship—because the president wanted it. But I knew from the outset that the only way the Mitchell could become the respected and prestigious scholarship that it has become was to be above that sort of thing. If we started awarding scholarships on the basis of one's connections, the program would have no integrity. Obviously, if you run a scholarship that is only a few years old, you would love the attention that a famous name can bring to your program. But that can never be a reason to select someone. There is not a higher bar for such a person, but we have to be in no doubt that the applicant moves forward on their own merit.

I explained to Senator Mitchell that Chelsea's boyfriend's application had been reviewed by several people. I did not envy him having to call the president, but I suggested that he tell the president that he himself had no say in the process, that all the candidates were carefully considered, but that Chelsea's boyfriend, while an impressive young man, was not selected as one of the twenty finalists. Mitchell said he would do so and for the momentary difficulty that put him in, I know he respected our unwillingness to be pressured.

That happened in November 2000. The next month, I was in Ireland with the first class of Mitchell Scholars when

President Clinton and Senator-elect Hillary Clinton were making their final visit of his presidency. When the US ambassador to Ireland, the former Wyoming governor Mike Sullivan, invited the Mitchell Scholars to a reception at his residence in the Phoenix Park to meet the president and First Lady, I was delighted they would have that opportunity. Sullivan would have had no reason to know what had just transpired.

I tried to hang back at the reception but did not escape being grabbed by a White House staffer who I assumed thought he was doing a nice thing by making sure I met the First Lady. It was immediately clear to me that she knew I was the person she viewed as responsible for Chelsea's boyfriend not getting the scholarship. For those few seconds, her eyes closed to a slit, the way they do when one is unhappy and sizing up a person. The Clintons were otherwise outwardly gracious and posed for photos with the Scholars and everyone present. But I sensed that all was not forgiven and forgotten.

Time passed, and, over the years, as a US senator for New York, Clinton did sign on to letters supporting the Scholarship. As someone who cared about Ireland and had many Scholars from, or currently residing in, her state, it would have been hard not to.

In late 2007, presidential candidate Hillary Clinton was pointing to the Northern Ireland peace process as evidence of her foreign policy experience during her time as First Lady. By March 2008, during a crucial period in the primaries, her exaggerations about her foreign policy credentials were fatal own goals.

Referring to a visit to Bosnia in the 1990s, Clinton claimed to have landed "under sniper fire" and said her party had to run "with our heads down to get into the vehicles." Video footage from the time showed otherwise. What made it worse was that this false claim came at the same time she was exaggerating her involvement in the Northern Ireland peace process when she was First Lady.

In his book about the 2008 campaign, *Redemption Song: Barack Obama: From Hope to Reality*, journalist Niall Stanage wrote, "Give Clinton her due. She visited Northern Ireland seven times between 1995 and 2004, she is very well-informed about its politics and its problems, and she, like her husband, is generally held in high esteem in Ireland." That assessment was accurate, and had Senator Clinton and her supporters not embellished her record, all would have been fine. There is no dispute that the Clintons care about Ireland.

New York Times columnist Maureen Dowd wrote of the exaggerations from the campaign trail in Ames, Iowa, on January 2, 2008: "By the time Bill and Hill are finished with you, you could be forgiven for thinking that she had personally forged the peace accord in Northern Ireland while socking away the $127 billion Clinton budget surplus and dodging bullets en route to ending ethnic cleansing in Bosnia."

It was often Clinton's allies who inflicted damage. The next day, a piece by Niall O'Dowd stated that the best thing that could happen for Ireland was if Hillary were elected. (In fact, had O'Dowd chosen to support a candidate based on their record on Irish issues, he would have gone with Senator Chris Dodd or Senator Joe Biden; both were candidates, and both had been substantively involved in the issues for much longer. But there was a lot of historical revisionism from those who saw personal advantage and access if Hillary became president.) Writing in the *Irish Times*, O'Dowd stated: "Senior staffers working for Senator Hillary Clinton were puzzled when their candidate recently insisted on taking a precious day off the presidential campaign trail in Iowa to return to Washington. She did so to meet with the Rev Ian Paisley and Martin McGuinness on their American trip, and to emphasise to the two leaders her commitment to Irish issues. Senior aides say no other foreign dignitaries would have enticed the highly disciplined candidate to forgo a day campaigning in the heat of battle for the Democratic nomination. But Northern Ireland and Ireland generally has come to occupy a very central place for the first potential woman president of the United States." That assertion was not only false, but it also demonstrates the need for a small but vocal number of Irish Americans to claim their own version of exceptionalism. Senator Clinton did not return to Washington *just* to meet the two Northern Ireland leaders, as O'Dowd led the reader to believe. Like the other candidates in Iowa (Senators Dodd, Biden, and Obama), she returned to the Capitol to vote on an important energy bill that dealt with renewables and ethanol—something voters in Iowa cared about. Senator Dodd also met with Paisley and McGuinness, something O'Dowd conveniently neglected to mention, even though Dodd played a much more substantive role in the Northern Ireland peace process than did the First Lady.

The day after O'Dowd's piece appeared, Terry McAuliffe, the chairman of Hillary's campaign, a longtime friend of the Clintons, and later governor of Virginia, made the outlandish claim on CNN's *American Morning* that "we would not have peace today had it not been for Hillary's hard work in Northern Ireland." The very next morning, on the same CNN program, when asked about her foreign policy qualifications, the candidate herself said, "I helped to bring peace to Northern Ireland."

At a campaign event in New Hampshire on January 7, former president Bill Clinton spoke of the recent visit of the Northern Ireland leaders who O'Dowd wrote of: "They came to the United States to see the president. They asked to see one other person—Hillary—to thank her for the independent role she played while I was president in the Irish peace process."

It was silly and untrue to suggest that Paisley and McGuinness wanted to see *only* President Bush and Senator

Clinton. A December 6 Associated Press story was entitled "Paisley Thanks Sen. Kennedy for Supporting Peace Talks in Northern Ireland." The article noted that Paisley "praised Kennedy's contributions to the peace process. . . ." And McGuinness said the process got vital support from a host of US political leaders and that "we thought it was important to come to express our gratitude to everybody here in the United States who contributed to the success of our process." Kennedy had set up a meeting that included other senators. The Northern Ireland leaders also met with Dodd and with members of the House of Representatives.

In January 2008, Senator Kennedy announced his support for Obama's candidacy. Kennedy spoke eloquently about Obama's message of hope and change and how he saw in Obama something of his brother Jack. This did not sit well with Niall O'Dowd, who wrote, "Kennedy probably felt that Obama represented the last throw of the dice for him in terms of the opportunity to influence a presidential race." More nonsense. To the extent Kennedy could influence a presidential race, he could have weighed in for Senator Clinton, an easy and politically safer bet. By all accounts, the Clintons were livid. In his 2013 book, *This Town*, Mark Leibovich wrote, "Bill's top post–White House aide, Doug Band, is keeping a list on his BlackBerry of all the people who screwed over the Clintons in the campaign and who are now, as they say, 'dead to us.'" He wrote that the Clinton insiders joked about what befell "the Clinton crossers," including Ted Kennedy, who was dying from a brain tumor.

In their book, *HRC*, Jonathan Allen and Amie Parnes wrote, "Clinton aides exulted in schadenfreude when their enemies faltered. Years later, they would joke about the fates of folks who they felt had betrayed them. 'Bill Richardson: investigated; John Edwards: disgraced by scandal; Chris Dodd: stepped down,' one said to another. 'Ted Kennedy,' the aide continued, lowering his voice to a whisper for the punch line, 'dead.'"

The unnecessary exaggerations about Hillary's role in Northern Ireland would snowball. By the middle of February, after the Super Tuesday primaries in several states, Obama was seen to be ahead; by late February, in advance of important March primaries in Texas and Ohio, Clinton launched an attack on Obama, questioning his wisdom and experience. By this point, evidence of her foreign policy experience was getting a closer look.

As the Irish issues person for the Obama campaign, it was my job to follow this. Personally, I was willing to let the first few exaggerations slide, as anyone can make a mistake, misremember, or gild the lily a bit, but the tall tales just kept growing, and finally, after this litany from several corners, including the candidate herself, I provided the campaign with the facts. As I had declined to be a public spokesperson for the campaign, Greg Craig, a former colleague in Kennedy's office and a foreign policy spokesperson for Obama, did the public running with a memo he released on March 11. Craig, who had also served as the director of Policy Planning in Bill Clinton's State Department, challenged Senator Clinton's claims of being a key player in foreign policy during her husband's presidency and noted, "It is a gross overstatement of the facts for her to claim even partial credit for bringing peace to Northern Ireland. She did travel to Northern Ireland, it is true. First Ladies often travel to places that are a focus of US foreign policy. But at no time did she play any role in the critical negotiations that ultimately produced the peace."

In an interview with O'Dowd's *Irish Voice* that appeared the following day, Senator Clinton continued with the fiction around the December visit of Paisley and McGuinness: "They met with the president, speaker, and me, which was very gratifying." As noted earlier, they met with several members of Congress.

On National Public Radio's *Morning Edition* with Steve Inskeep on March 13, the candidate was forced to begin walking back from the exaggerations. Trying to deflect by accusing her opponents of "nitpicking," she said, "What I was was part of a team . . . I wasn't sitting at the negotiating table but the role I played was instrumental . . . when Ian Paisley and Martin McGuinness came . . . I think they met with the leadership of Congress, with the President and with me and they thanked me publicly for the role that I had played."

Northern Ireland political leader John Hume was the only person actually involved who was overly generous in saying the First Lady played a "pivotal role" in the peace process, but he couldn't give specific examples and could say only that she "visited" and "gave support." When the Obama team asked me what was up with that seeming endorsement, I explained that those of us who worked closely with John knew he had been having memory difficulties for some time. I told the campaign to just let John's comments slide, as there was nothing to be gained by embarrassing the ailing Nobel Prize winner. The campaign team agreed and said nothing to publicly refute Hume. John's incredible wife, Pat, has since publicly disclosed that, as a result of a 1999 medical procedure, John has suffered memory difficulties.

Senator Kennedy was also incredulous about the credit Senator Clinton was taking. He rang me and jokingly asked if he'd forgotten her involvement. He said that Michael Duffy from *Time* magazine had been onto him about the issue, and Kennedy asked if, because I knew the minutiae, I would ring him. I agreed to talk with Duffy on background and did so. Jean Kennedy Smith, the senator's sister and President Clinton's ambassador to Ireland during the critical years of the process, said on the record in Duffy's March 13 article that the

First Lady had nothing to do with the negotiations: "As far as anything political went, there was nothing as far as I know, nothing to do with negotiations."

Jonathan Powell, Tony Blair's chief of staff, who worked in the British embassy in Washington at the time, told Dominic Lawson of the *Independent* "that he wouldn't comment on Mrs. Clinton's claims, 'because I don't want to tell a lie'"; Powell's own book on the negotiations didn't mention her in any substantive way.

In 1997, *Irish Times* journalist Conor O'Clery wrote the first detailed book on the US role in Northern Ireland as it related to the Adams visa and what followed. At the time, Senator Kennedy and I agreed to be of only minor assistance to the former Washington correspondent because the process was at a delicate stage; we felt there was some risk in patting ourselves on the back and possibly alienating Northern Ireland's Unionist politicians. Kennedy was very willing to choose policy over publicity. Niall O'Dowd and Nancy Soderberg were major sources for O'Clery's book, so one would think that if the First Lady had played any real role, they would have said so, as would anyone else O'Clery interviewed. In O'Clery's *Daring Diplomacy: Clinton's Secret Search for Peace in Ireland*, Hillary Clinton is mentioned five times, but there are no references to her playing any role; she is referred to merely as accompanying her husband.

In a March 2008 Associated Press piece, Senator Mitchell was quoted saying, "She was one of the many people who participated in encouraging women to get involved, not the only one," which was in keeping with his 1999 account of the peace process, *Making Peace*, in which Senator Mitchell did not indicate that the First Lady had any substantive role in the peace process.

It is worth noting that while President Clinton proclaimed his wife's significance in the Northern Ireland peace process during the 2008 campaign, in his own 2004 memoir, *My Life*, within thirty-one pages of references to Northern Ireland, he did not indicate that his wife played any role in the process. President Clinton mentions her twice, and both references are about her accompanying him to Northern Ireland. He didn't even mention her bringing women together in Northern Ireland, which during the campaign the Clintons suggested was so important. And when I worked closely with the White House on the peace process, no one there said anything about the First Lady being involved or expressing strong views. (Such conversations are not unusual between staffers when a politician's spouse is inserting themselves in an issue.)

In addition to the Obama campaign, others who did call it straight included former SDLP politician and author Brian Feeney, who pointedly wrote, "The road to peace was carefully documented, and she wasn't on it." David Trimble, former Ulster Unionist party leader and first minister of Northern Ireland, told Toby Harnden of the *Telegraph* that it was a "wee bit silly" for Clinton to be exaggerating the part she played. Former journalist John O'Farrell, who had covered US politicians' visits to Northern Ireland, told the *Boston Globe*, "Her heart was always in the right place, no one doubted that. But the idea of her bringing together fiercely opposed combatants is a considerable exaggeration." Kevin Cullen, longtime astute observer of Northern Ireland for the *Boston Globe*, wrote, "It all depends on how you define help. . . . Using her logic, you could say that" Van Morrison, who sang at the 1995 lighting of the Christmas tree at Belfast City Hall, "did as much as Hillary Clinton to bring peace to Northern Ireland."

In his book *The Blair Years: The Alastair Campbell Diaries*, Campbell covers 1994 through 2003. While the prime minister's former communications director gives considerable attention to Northern Ireland, there is no reference to Hillary Clinton with regard to a role in the peace process.

In the several pages Sidney Blumenthal writes about Northern Ireland in his 2003 book, *The Clinton Wars*, the longtime confidant of the Clintons mentions Hillary twice. The first reference claims that when she visited Northern Ireland in the fall of 1997, "the peace negotiations . . . were hitting a rough patch at this juncture, but Hillary's work helped push them forward a bit. . . . In Belfast, Hillary delivered a speech at the University of Ulster in memory of Joyce McCartan, a community activist. . . ." But in Toby Harnden's contemporaneous report of her visit for the *Telegraph* on November 1, 1997, he wrote, "Mrs. Clinton steered clear of any overt political statements and stressed the contribution ordinary people could make to peace." He further noted that when a sixteen-year-old boy "departed from the script and asked about the issues of 'political prisoners' and the decommissioning of terrorist weapons, Mrs. Clinton smiled and nodded and the conversation was shifted swiftly to the experiences of disabled people in Ulster."

Blumenthal's second reference referred to "another mistake" Hillary made when running for the Senate. When asked about New York's St. Patrick's Day parade, she said she'd hoped to march in it, not realizing it was contentious because the organizers refused to allow gays and lesbians to march. Blumenthal neglected to mention that in 2000, when running for the Senate against Rudy Giuliani, candidate Hillary Clinton marched in the parade, to the unhappiness of the LGBT community.

In Mo Mowlam's book, *Momentum*, while there are references to bringing women together, the former secretary of state for Northern Ireland didn't suggest any role for Clinton other than "giving women in N. Ireland encouragement and support."

On March 9, 2008, Maureen Dowd wrote in the *New York Times* of "Hillary's risible claim that she has far more national security experience" than Obama. "Having a first lady tea in Belfast is not equivalent to bringing peace to Northern Ireland," noted Dowd.

Most tellingly, if her role in Northern Ireland was so significant, why didn't Hillary Clinton mention that in her 2003 book *Living History*? In the five-hundred-page autobiography, she mentions Northern Ireland on several occasions but never suggests she played an instrumental role in ending the conflict. Her recollection of her role in the mid-1990s grew with her political aspirations.

Many saw Clinton's exaggerations about her record as doing great damage to her campaign. Obama's fortunes would continue to rise, her campaign would continue to falter, and she would concede in less than three months. My role in all of this, providing facts to the Obama campaign, would not be forgotten in Hillary World.

The Irish Government, Caught between Barack and a Hard Place

Given President Clinton's role in the Northern Ireland peace process, many reasonably believed that Hillary, a known entity, would bring that connection with her if she became president. But Taoiseach Bertie Ahern, someone who truly was instrumental in the peace process, made a rare political misstep by seeming to wade into the issue during the 2008 St. Patrick's Day festivities.

While the implosion of the Irish economy later in 2008 tarnished the former taoiseach's reputation, history will reflect his dogged commitment to achieving peace in Northern Ireland. Ahern's mother died during the most crucial, final days of the negotiations, and all involved remember how he left her funeral to go straight back to the negotiations. I will always be grateful to Ahern because he immediately grasped the potential for the Mitchell Scholarship program and the US-Ireland Alliance and threw his support behind them.

In March 2008, the taoiseach arrived in Washington under a great deal of pressure at home, and he would resign later that month. Ahern flew into Washington, DC, on Sunday, March 16, after visiting Scranton, Pennsylvania. The following morning, he met with Senator Clinton and spoke by phone, for the first time, with Senator Obama.

After the call, Denis McDonough, Obama's foreign policy adviser, let me know that the conversation happened but that Obama boarded a plane just after, so Denis would have to wait until later in the day to get a readout on the conversation. As I had written Obama's talking points, I had a fair understanding of what he likely said on the call, but I didn't know what the taoiseach said. In the throes of the primaries, I didn't expect that it would have been much more than a courtesy call.

That evening, as I was on my way to the annual St. Patrick's Day party at the residence of the Irish ambassador in Washington, word was coming to me that the main television station in Ireland, RTE, was reporting that the taoiseach was defending Senator Clinton in the row over her involvement in the peace process. Concerning was the report that the taoiseach was suggesting that Obama, in their conversation that morning, took his point—i.e., agreed that Clinton was being unfairly criticized.

The RTE clip showed the taoiseach saying, "And I have to say in my conversation this morning, that was totally acknowledged by Senator Obama. So, so I mean I'm not gonna get into the politics of this but I think for anyone to try to question the Clintons' huge support and start trying to nitpick . . ." From reading Ahern's comments alone, it was unclear *what* was "totally acknowledged" by Senator Obama. Prior to his comments, the RTE reporter said, "The Obama campaign has been questioning Senator Clinton's involvement in the peace process. But Mr. Ahern said she had played a significant and important role." As the reporter said "significant" and "important," it was unclear whether those were Ahern's words, but Ahern's use of the word "nitpick" was the word Senator Clinton had used on NPR.

I read the transcript just before walking into the party where the taoiseach and his advisers would be. Before going inside, I rang McDonough, let him know about the RTE report, and told him we needed to know what Obama said in that conversation. Denis said he had spoken to Obama in the interim and that he had said no such thing; in fact, he said nothing about Senator Clinton in his conversation with the taoiseach.

Inside the residence, I sought out the Irish ambassador, Michael Collins, and Gerry Hickey, a close adviser of Ahern whom I knew and with whom I had a good relationship. I told them what RTE was reporting and that this was a problem. While the campaign did not wish to contradict the taoiseach, neither could it let stand the inaccurate impression that Obama agreed that Clinton was unfairly treated on the issue of her role in the peace process. I told them McDonough confirmed that Obama said no such thing. Collins and Hickey said they weren't with the taoiseach when the call happened, but Hickey walked across the room and pulled the taoiseach aside to ask him. Hickey returned, saying that Ahern only said that Hillary was supportive, and that Obama didn't have a problem with what he said. That was pretty vague—did Ahern simply make a statement, and he then read no response from Obama as acceptance or agreement?

We next found the taoiseach's press secretary, Eoghan O Neachtain, who was with the taoiseach during the phone conversation and had a transcript. According to O Neachtain, the taoiseach said that of course Hillary wasn't at the negotiations but that she was supportive. That tracked with David Falchek's

piece in the *Scranton Times* that quoted the taoiseach as saying, "She was the first lady of the United States, not a party
leader in Northern Ireland. . . . No one would expect her to get
into the nitty-gritty of the process." The taoiseach was obviously free to say what he liked about Clinton, but regardless
of whether he said her role was supportive or important, he
could not speak for Obama and suggest that he agreed that the
criticism of her was unfair.

While Collins and Hickey immediately saw the importance of the nuance and the potential seriousness of the situation given all that had transpired on this issue, O Neachtain
was cavalier. He said that it wouldn't become an issue if Obama
didn't make it an issue. I told him Obama would not be making
it an issue but that the Clinton camp would have a field day
with it.

McDonough later told me he would ring O Neachtain to
impress upon him the seriousness of the matter and that the
Irish needed to sort this out so as not to put the Obama campaign in the position of having to contradict the taoiseach.
Denis said afterward that O Neachtain promised he would
contact RTE to correct any misimpression and told him the
taoiseach was less effusive in his praise of Senator Clinton than
was being reported. He reiterated that the taoiseach said she
was there on the trips and was active with women's groups,
and then he asked rhetorically, "Was she at the negotiating
table? You all know that she was not."

The story died after that. As the Clinton team normally
would have run with this seeming endorsement by the Irish
prime minister and they didn't, I suspected that someone on
the Irish side not only told RTE but also warned the Clinton
campaign that if they pushed that story, both the taoiseach and
Clinton would be embarrassed.

Ahern would get himself into more hot water during that
visit to the US, but this time for telling it accurately. A few

months earlier, I wrote an opinion piece in the *Irish Times* explaining why the Irish who were illegally in the US wouldn't get a "special deal." In the *Irish Times* on March 18, Mark Hennessy and Denis Staunton reported from Washington that the taoiseach, "speaking following White House talks with US president George Bush, said an amnesty solely for the Irish was 'not on,'" and RTE reported that after the St. Patrick's Day luncheon on Capitol Hill, Ahern said, "People talking up the prospects of such a deal were 'sitting in the bar talking nonsense.'" This infuriated Niall O'Dowd, who was constantly suggesting there was a special deal just around the corner.

Shortly after St. Patrick's Day, I invited senior Obama adviser Tony Lake to join me for lunch with Ambassador Collins to assure Collins that the Irish would have an ear in the Obama administration. I told Lake that Collins would argue for a special envoy for Northern Ireland, a rank first established for George Mitchell and that continued under the Bush administration. A year earlier, we put out an Obama statement saying there would be an envoy, but so much progress had been made since then that it was now hard to see a need for one. When I had earlier discussed this with Collins and tried to tease out exactly why this was needed, he said that Ireland wanted one because it made them feel special, but there was no substantive reason. Clinton said she would name a special envoy, but was one necessary? It was an easy thing to say during a campaign, but would it even stick with her? Madeleine Albright, a Hillary supporter and Bill Clinton's former secretary of state, had a new book out at the time in which Northern Ireland was mentioned only once. That wasn't surprising, in that Albright hadn't been heavily involved in the issue. During Bill Clinton's administration, the important work on Northern Ireland was handled by Lake, Soderberg, Holl, and later Jim Steinberg—all in the White House. Albright did write about special envoys in general but saw Senator Mitchell's role for Northern Ireland as the exception. There was a sense in the State Department that special envoys were becoming too numerous, and therefore not so special.

Ireland was at a crossroads. The country did not need constant US attention and hand-holding. The politicians and diplomats knew it, but it was hard to let go. The Irish could be insecure when it came to attention paid, particularly vis-à-vis the British government. Collins had previously told me that he understood that US government funding for the International Fund for Ireland (aid for Northern Ireland and the border counties) was going to end, that he expected the American Ireland Fund wouldn't be in existence much longer, that the ground was shifting, but the government's concern was just the fear that the US would go cold turkey on Ireland. Intellectually, they understood but were nervous—it was really more about the optics than the substance.

Tony and I had lunch with Collins at the Monocle, a Capitol Hill restaurant that was popular due to its close proximity to the Senate office buildings, not to mention the tasty salted bread. While I didn't expect the Irish would publicly correct that misstatement by the taoiseach, Michael confirmed that they had spoken to Senator Clinton's people and made clear that suggesting that Obama had agreed with the taoiseach on Hillary and Northern Ireland would be a mistake.

Tony and I said that no one was saying the taoiseach couldn't say nice things about Senator Clinton; he just shouldn't involve himself in a US campaign, and he especially shouldn't mischaracterize Obama's views.

As predicted, the main issue Collins raised was that of a special envoy. He suggested that it was not so much about the title as it was about knowing there is a senior go-to person for Ireland in an Obama administration. While we were still months away from the election, I found it a bit premature to make any decisions but did agree that there should be a person, regardless of title, who served such a purpose. In the Clinton years, the Ireland brief resided in the White House; with President Bush, it was in the office of Policy Planning in the Department of State. Tony and I were on the same page, and he told Collins that we weren't for or against an envoy but that it was something we could review after the election. Tony assured him the Irish would have an ear in an Obama administration.

Lake reinforced Obama's unifying nature and his dislike of ethnic politics. Niall O'Dowd had a go at Samantha Power after the *Sunday Business Post* reported in January that the Ireland-born adviser to the president said, in talking about Obama's relationship with the Irish, "Obama did not want to peel off groups—such as the Irish and women—and start pandering to them. She said he preferred to deal with the issues as they affected everyone in the country, and not pigeonhole them into categories." One of the reasons I admired Obama was for his vision of a united America as opposed to one sliced and diced—the vision, which first brought him to national prominence when he spoke at the 2004 Democratic Convention in Boston. When I asked Collins if anyone was thinking about these changes, he said there was to be a June meeting in Ireland to discuss how Ireland could be relevant in the US. Lake said the Irish were relevant, but rather they should just think about how they would adjust to the changes.

Bill Clinton, a No-Show in Belfast

In the *Irish Examiner* on March 15, 2008, Shaun Connolly, political correspondent in New York, wrote that, two nights previously at an event in New York, Bill Clinton "launched an angry attack on Barack Obama for attempting to 'ridicule' his wife's role in the Good Friday Agreement when she was first lady."

In April 2008, the US-Ireland Alliance would stage a major event in Belfast to mark the tenth anniversary of the Northern Ireland peace agreement. In the throes of the US presidential campaign and the stories about Hillary's role in the process, Bill Clinton, after first agreeing to take part in the event, withdrew just weeks before.

Two years earlier, the then director of our scholarship program, Mary Lou Hartman, had the great idea of marking the tenth anniversary with Senator Mitchell in Belfast. We invited the main negotiators to participate and gather on one stage to reminisce. The plan was to have an audience of largely twenty- to thirty-year-olds. It would be a reunion of the Mitchell Scholars, and we invited their Northern Ireland and Irish peers, as well as people in Belfast, to give an inspirational look back and forward.

We quickly received generous financial support from Chuck Feeney's Atlantic Philanthropies and Irish property developers Noel Smyth and Derek Quinlan. With Senator Mitchell's agreement to participate, we began to plan and issue invitations more than a year in advance of the event. In addition to the Northern Ireland leaders, we invited British prime minister Tony Blair, Bill Clinton, and Taoiseach Bertie Ahern. In May 2007, we put out the first press release about our plans.

In October 2007, Kris Balderston, the longtime aide to both Clintons, called to ask if I would help with something. Bill Clinton had promised Martin McGuinness and Peter Robinson that he would help on the issue of suicide prevention in Northern Ireland. (After the peace agreement in Northern Ireland, suicides had increased. *The Detail*, the Belfast investigative online journal, found that between 1998 and 2012, nearly as many people in Northern Ireland died by suicide since the signing of the Good Friday Agreement as had died during the Troubles.) Kris let me know that if I could help deliver something for Clinton on this, it would make it more likely that he would accept the invitation to our event. While I didn't really see it as my job to help the former president deliver on promises he'd made, I said I would see if I could help. On the one hand, I thought that, as Bill Clinton was much more connected than I was, he could surely do this without my help. On the other hand, suicide prevention is an important cause, and if I could help in some way, it would be a win-win. At no time did it enter my mind that because I was helping the Obama campaign, I should not help President Clinton. Balderston approached me before Hillary's claims about her role in Northern Ireland became an issue.

In late November, I was in Dublin to cook Thanksgiving dinner for the Mitchell Scholars on the island. For Americans abroad, Thanksgiving seems like the loneliest of holidays because it is such a family gathering at home, and also because it is a holiday that obviously is not celebrated outside the US. Each year, good friends in Ireland, Paul Hayes and Mary Calpin, invite us to their home, and we cook for fifteen to twenty people.

While in Dublin, I met with Noel Smyth, the Dublin property developer whose company, Alburn, was a sponsor of our upcoming Belfast event. I knew that Noel had a personal experience with suicide and that he founded an all-island suicide prevention organization called Turn the Tide, or 3Ts. When I told Smyth of Clinton's promise to McGuinness and Robinson, he generously offered to pull together a suicide prevention fund-raiser in Dublin the night after our event in Belfast. He said he would also ask Ahern and Blair to attend, and I asked Senator Mitchell, who quickly agreed to participate.

I let Balderston know of Smyth's offer. This did indeed seem to move the needle with Clinton, and I visited his Harlem office in the midst of a snowstorm on December 13, 2007, to discuss logistics with his staff. But a bigger storm was on the horizon in the form of the issue of Hillary's role in the peace process.

After much back-and-forth, on February 21, 2008, I heard from Alvarez von Gustedt, a foreign policy adviser at the Clinton Foundation, confirming that Clinton would travel to Belfast to participate in our event and the suicide prevention dinner. A few days later, we learned that Tony Blair could not be in Belfast on our date but could make the suicide prevention dinner the following night in Dublin. Bertie Ahern, like Senator Mitchell, was in for both.

Although all was on schedule on March 14 and plans were being made for the former president, five days later, I received a call from his scheduler, Tascha, informing me that he would now not be going to Ireland because "his schedule has changed." I sought an explanation from Tascha, who suddenly was brief and vague, only confirming that his "schedule no longer permits him to travel to Northern Ireland."

Given what had just transpired in the campaign, I immediately suspected this was payback for the fact that Senator Clinton's overreach on her role in the peace process had been called out. While it was no secret that on my own time I was helping the Obama campaign, I was not a public representative and had made no public comments. But the Clinton camp would have known that the level of detail provided would have come from me.

Having no evidence other than my own intuition, I was prepared to accept the line that Bill Clinton's schedule had changed. But what stoked my immediate suspicion was the Clinton office's unwillingness to provide us with a simple quote from the former president. It would be a very easy, and typical thing, for staff to provide a quote from him along the lines of, "It will be a great event and I deeply regret that I'm unable to be there." Despite my asking several Clinton staffers for a quote prior to my releasing the news that he was out, not one person responded.

On March 20, we put out a short and sweet press release stating that the former president had "canceled his trip due to a change in his schedule."

The next day, Larry Rohter of the *New York Times* contacted me saying that he was writing a story about the upcoming tenth anniversary of the Belfast Agreement and how that was playing out against the backdrop of the Democratic primaries. Rohter, whom I didn't know and had never been in contact with before, told me that he was "getting rumblings from the Irish-American community here in New York" that the former president was not participating in our event "because of disagreements with Obama supporters about Mrs. Clinton's role in the original talks." Confirmation of what I'd suspected.

Off the record, I explained to Rohter the background with O'Dowd, who I expected was the likely source of this story. On the record, I told him the facts: the US-Ireland Alliance is a nonpartisan organization that does not endorse any candidates, and I was helping the campaign as a volunteer and had not been public about that. This Belfast event had been in the planning for more than two years and had nothing to do with the US presidential campaign. In Rohter's March 22 piece in the *New York Times*, he mentioned that Greg Craig and I had worked for Kennedy and were now supporting Obama. He wrote that President Clinton's withdrawal from our Belfast event was "adding a new element of intrigue to the controversy over exactly what role his wife, Senator Hillary Rodham Clinton, played in that peace process."

Whoever thought that a *New York Times* story, bringing up the issue yet again, could help Hillary Clinton clearly hadn't thought that through. The smart thing would have been to let the story be that Bill Clinton had a scheduling conflict; otherwise he looked petty—he was backing out of a tenth-anniversary event he had committed to that involved future leaders and those he worked with in Belfast because it was meant to be payback for a woman who wasn't exactly a household name.

We would have welcomed the former president's participation, given his critical role in the process. I had done everything asked of me, including arranging a fund-raising dinner for suicide prevention to fulfill his commitment—a dinner he also dropped out of by canceling his trip. What annoyed me was that his team had me put down a nonrefundable deposit on a block of hotel rooms in Belfast that I couldn't get back. Although the costs incurred were flagged for the Clinton team, they never offered to reimburse.

Our Belfast event was a huge success—for the young leaders, and as a reunion for the peace negotiators—and it garnered press attention around the world. Ahern, Mitchell, and Blair all participated in the suicide fund-raiser, so all went ahead as planned.

And where was the former president when he was originally meant to be in Belfast? At an event in Manhattan, where he was being honored for his role in the peace process by the Emerald Isle Immigration Center and the Brehon Law Society. Marion McKeone, an Irish journalist who was covering the campaign for Ireland's *Sunday Tribune*, called the event "two hours of stupefying pojiggery and begobbery" with "excruciating speeches bookended by excruciating speeches." McKeone noted that, on the same night, Hillary made an appearance at "the grandiosely titled Irish-American Presidential Forum 2008. The entire event, from the tiny, sweaty venue with its chintzy decor and plastic flowers to the bawdy warm-up act, seemed to belong to another era, an era when the hat was being passed around for Noraid at New York hostelries." McKeone noted that Clinton "was summoned to the event by its organisers to answer six questions about what she would do for

Ireland if she were elected president. Given that it's a big 'if,' she can afford to be generous, throwing in a peace envoy, bonds, a few summits and no sooner would the ink be dry on her inaugural pledge than she'd be on the plane to Belfast. Then it's onto reminiscing about the peace process. Mindful of the flak over Bosnia and other alleged distortions, Clinton is careful not to overstate her hand. . . ."

Hillary Clinton's memory issues involving events in Northern Ireland would continue when she became Obama's secretary of state. During an October 2009 visit to Northern Ireland, in a speech to members of the Northern Ireland Assembly, she talked about her first visit to Belfast as First Lady in November 1995: "We stayed at the Europa Hotel . . . even though then there were sections boarded up because of damage from bombs." Niall Stanage, writing for the *Daily Beast*, asked, "What is it about Hillary Clinton and conflict zones?" He recalled her campaign assertions and noted that her comments before the Northern Ireland Assembly had "the potential to resurrect questions about whether Clinton has a tendency to over-dramatize her foreign endeavors." The hotel owner and general manager confirmed for Stanage that the last explosion to damage the hotel happened two-and-a-half years before the Clinton visit, and the place was therefore not boarded up when she visited.

Payback

Barack Obama was elected as president, and trouble was on the horizon for our George J. Mitchell Scholarship program when Hillary became his secretary of state.

The Mitchell had become one of the most desired scholarships for future American leaders. Recipients not only have to be academically excellent, but they must have strong records of service and leadership as well. Even though the prestigious Rhodes Scholarship has been around a lot longer and was much better funded by an endowment from the person for whom it was named, applicants are turning down Rhodes interviews for the Mitchell.

For more than a decade, the State Department provided a little less than $500,000 annually for the program (a small amount in terms of State's budget, but a large amount for our small nonprofit). That support was forthcoming in both the Bill Clinton and George W. Bush administrations, because of the encouragement of many in Congress. Besides being popular with students, US and Irish universities, and the Irish government, the program is lean—we've kept the budget nearly flat throughout its twenty-year existence.

It was therefore hard to understand why funding for the Mitchell Scholarship program was totally eliminated by Secretary Clinton's State Department at a time when she was complaining that too few Americans were studying abroad.

The *Daily Beast* called Melanne Verveer, a longtime friend of Hillary Clinton's, Hillary's "secret weapon." Verveer served as the First Lady's chief of staff during the Bill Clinton White House years. In 2009, Secretary of State Clinton made her the first ever ambassador-at-large and director of the State Department's office for Global Women's Issues.

Her title would not suggest that Verveer should be paying attention to a scholarship to Ireland, but Verveer was also a defender of Hillary Clinton's exaggerated role in Northern Ireland during the 2008 campaign. I don't know Verveer. I don't think I ever met her. But she knows me. In 2011, Mary Lou Hartman, former director of the Mitchell Scholarship program, bumped into Verveer, who made clear that I was persona non grata because of my role in exposing the First Lady's non-role in the peace negotiations. Just months later, the State Department informed us they were totally eliminating all funding for the Mitchell Scholarship program in the next State Department budget.

This also occurred when Ann Stock was the head of the bureau in the Department of State that oversaw Mitchell Scholarship funding (the Bureau of Educational and Cultural Affairs). Stock ran the bureau from 2010 to 2013 and has a relationship with Verveer going back to when they were both in the Bill Clinton White House—Stock was the White House social secretary and another person close to Clinton.

Department officials told us they were eliminating the Mitchell because Europe wasn't a priority and they were looking to save money. But that didn't add up.

There are a lot of zeros here, so let's put this in perspective. In the year in question, the Obama administration's budget proposal for the Department of State/USAID was $51.6 billion. (As an aside for those who mistakenly believe the United States spends a lot of money on State/foreign aid, we don't. That was just 1 percent of the federal budget.) The ECA Bureau received around $550 million of that for scholarships and exchanges. The Mitchell Scholarship had been receiving less than $500,000 over the years. That is less than 0.1 percent of the ECA budget. And given that we had so much Capitol Hill support, no Republican opposition and were receiving funds from the Irish government and private sources—something State regularly said they wanted to see with programs—the Mitchell should have easily continued to receive funding.

Using the State Department's own figures, the cost of a Mitchell was no more than the cost of a Fulbright Scholarship, and possibly as little as half that price. And the Fulbright, the department's flagship program, is global and not unique to the island of Ireland. The Mitchell was, and remains, the most prestigious scholarship for study in Ireland. The elimination of funding for the Mitchell was not about money.

There is no disputing a deprioritization of Europe in the Obama administration with Clinton at the helm in the State Department. In October 2011, Secretary of State Clinton wrote a very lengthy piece for *Foreign Policy* entitled "America's Pacific Century." The title said it all. She wrote, "One of the most important tasks of American statecraft over the next decade will therefore be to lock in a substantially increased investment—diplomatic, economic, strategic, and otherwise—in the Asia-Pacific region." And while noting that "our post-World War II commitment to building a comprehensive and lasting transatlantic network of institutions and relationships has paid off many times over," the time had come "for the United States to make similar investments as a Pacific power."

In the *Washington Post* on May 30, 2014, Walter Russell Mead asked, "Was Hillary Clinton a good secretary of state?" He described the focus of her worldview as being on Asia but suggested that the "pivot" to Asia may not have only "reinvigorated America's Pacific alliances but also elicited a more aggressive China" and "encouraged Putin to think that the United States was taking its eye off Russia's revisionist ambitions."

President Obama maintained this focus throughout his presidency. In *The Atlantic* in April 2016, Jeffrey Goldberg wrote an extensive article based on his interview with the president. He wrote that Obama "is fixated on turning America's attention to Asia," and "Europe, about which he is unromantic, is a source of global stability that requires, to his occasional annoyance, American hand-holding."

I never understood why pivoting to Asia meant we had to lessen our commitment to Europe. These things are not mutually exclusive, and in a variety of ways, including mass migration and Brexit, the Obama administration would come to realize Europe could not be ignored. The pivot was real, but that, and payback, are not mutually exclusive.

Journalist Carol Morello wrote in the *Washington Post* on March 20, 2018, that President Trump's State Department had taken the name off a scholarship named for Hillary Clinton: The article said that Clinton spokesperson Nick Merrill called the name deletion "a disgrace." He went on to say that "cutting programs that support students is bad enough. Doing it to be vindictive to a former Secretary of State is beyond the pale, and sends a terrible message about American values." Remember, in February 2012, the State Department, under Secretary of State Hillary Clinton, eliminated all funding for the George J. Mitchell Scholarship program. That was less than $500,000 a year. One of the alleged reasons for that was tight budgets. The *Washington Post* piece said that, *in the same year,* the State Department established "the Fulbright-Clinton Fellowship" at a cost of more than $800,000 a year. Clinton's spokesperson was outraged that Trump was eliminating something named for a Clinton, but he had no such qualms about eliminating funding for something named after Senator George Mitchell?

For the Irish American activists who argued what a great friend Hillary would be for Ireland, there must have been great disappointment, though those who were still hoping for personal gain from a possible future Clinton presidency would never say that. Clinton did not name a special envoy, she did nothing to support a "special deal" for the Irish illegally in the US, and US support for the International Fund for Ireland dwindled when she was secretary of state. I don't disagree with any of those moves; the passage of time made all those things inevitable. But I never had any illusions about where Ireland would rank, no matter whether Obama or Clinton had become president.

But cutting the Mitchell funding made the least sense, and every excuse the secretary's political appointees served up was easily shot down.

When President Obama appointed Hillary Clinton as his secretary of state, the move was very much seen as a matter of keeping your enemy close. Much has been written about the rivalry between the Clinton State Department and the Obama White House. Over the last couple of decades, the White House has taken on more of a foreign policy role. In 2015, it was estimated that the size of Obama's National Security Council staff (the White House foreign policy branch) had grown to four hundred, which, according to the *Washington Post*, was "about twice the size it was at the end of the George W. Bush Administration."

Unfortunately, the Mitchell Scholarship program never rose to the level of importance to warrant the White House bothering to override Clinton. They were happy enough to leave the small stuff to her. They had to pick their battles, and this would not be one of them.

Despite all of this, in case you are wondering, I voted for Hillary Clinton in 2016. I wasn't thrilled to be doing so, but to vote for Donald Trump would have been petty and counter to my core values. I'm only sorry Clinton and those around her didn't equally take the high road when it came to funding the Mitchell Scholarship program.

An Emerald That Wasn't So Green

While serving as an issues adviser, I avoided the ethnic outreach part of political campaigns. My experience was that this frequently involved groups and individuals demanding silly things merely to claim that they got a candidate to say x or do y. I'm not talking about the big, important issues of policy. I'm referring to the endless requests for small things that feel like extortion for support. During the 2008 campaign, I was regularly asked about this or that demand from a handful of Irish

Americans. Given what was going on in our country and the world, 99 percent of the requests did not merit any candidate's attention.

At one point, the Obama campaign was being pushed to name check William Thompson, the then comptroller of New York City. Of all the many individuals who were involved in Irish issues, Thompson would not have been high on the list. It was as if those who wanted him mentioned were trying to grasp for an African American with some involvement in Ireland. The suggestion of Thompson came from labor leader Joe Jamison; Mairtin O'Muilleoir, publisher of *The Irish Echo*, later Northern Ireland's finance minister and an investor in the *Irish Central* tabloid; and the 1960s activist Tom Hayden. The push for this was relentless. Perhaps some were seeking to ingratiate themselves with the person they thought would be the next mayor of New York City. They wanted Thompson mentioned in connection with his creation of something referred to as the "Emerald Fund." I didn't know Thompson, but I refused to put that in a statement because there was no evidence that there was any there there when it came to the Emerald Fund.

I remembered when the Fund was announced, because the then first minister of Northern Ireland, Ian Paisley, and the deputy first minister, Martin McGuinness, flew to New York for the announcement. It was April 2008, and I was in Belfast, where the US-Ireland Alliance was hosting the event marking the tenth anniversary of the Belfast Agreement. Paisley never supported the peace agreement and was never planning to be part of our event. Sinn Fein's Martin McGuinness and Gerry Adams were both to participate, but when the New York opportunity arose, Adams remained part of our event while McGuinness went to New York with Paisley.

The Northern Ireland government put out a press release at the time stating that "William C. Thompson Jr. Comptroller of the City of New York who is Chief Investment Advisor of the New York City Pension Funds which currently hold assets of $110 billion" announced "that trustees of the fund were committing $150 million to the Emerald Investment Development Fund LP, a private equity fund that will total some $750 million and will target infrastructure investment projects."

After returning from Northern Ireland, I had lunch with RTE reporter Robert Shortt at a restaurant called the Front Page in Dupont Circle. We were skeptical of the fund because we didn't see how there would be a good return on investment from building Northern Ireland infrastructure. Our suspicions proved true.

A year later, in May 2009, Tom Robbins wrote in the *Village Voice* that a major beneficiary of the Fund was a friend of Thompson's who got a $3 million fee. In March 2011, in the Northern Ireland online investigative magazine *The Detail*, John Breslin declared, "Not a single cent of the promised money has been invested. The fund is dead."

In 2013, when Thompson was running for mayor of New York, the *New York Times'* Michael Powell cited the Fund in questioning Thompson's fitness to manage the city's funds. I was relieved we hadn't succumbed to the pressure to have Obama applaud Thompson in 2008.

Taxes and American Companies in Ireland

Another area of misinformation during the campaign involved the candidates' positions on the issue of American corporations that avoid US taxes by being taxed as residents in Ireland.

The US tax code allows domestic companies to defer taxes on "unrepatriated income." That means that US companies don't pay tax on the revenue earned by their overseas subsidiaries unless and until that money is brought back to the US.

Because the US corporate tax rate was 35 percent versus 12.5 percent in Ireland, you don't have to be an accountant to know where you'd rather pay taxes. Increasingly, American companies have established entities in Ireland. Some have made Ireland their global headquarters. While Ireland's young, educated, and English-speaking workforce is a bonus, there is little dispute that Ireland's attractiveness rests heavily on the tax incentive.

During every election cycle in the US, politicians running for office told voters they would close loopholes. Democrats tended to say they would find a way so companies couldn't do this, and Republicans advocated dropping the US tax rate to compete with countries like Ireland. This issue always causes concern in Ireland, as the country relies heavily on foreign direct investment from the US.

Niall O'Dowd, supporting Hillary Clinton, repeatedly told the Irish that when it came to the tax issue, Obama would be worse for Ireland. In truth, in 2008, there was no daylight between Obama and Clinton on the issue.

In a speech in Spartanburg, South Carolina, on November 3, 2007, Obama vowed, "When I am president, I will end the tax giveaways to companies that ship our jobs overseas, and I will put the money in the pockets of working Americans, and seniors, and homeowners who deserve a break."

Sixteen days later, in Knoxville, Tennessee, Clinton said, "And we are going to finally close the tax loopholes and stop giving tax breaks to companies that ship jobs overseas. Enough with outsourcing American jobs using taxpayer dollars."

Such statements were repeated throughout the campaign by both sides. O'Dowd was spinning another false narrative of how Obama would uniquely be bad for the Irish economy, an assertion he would repeat on Marian Finucane's RTE Irish radio program on March 22, 2008. O'Dowd didn't mention that Senator Clinton's views were identical. The new Irish

prime minister, Brian Cowen, made clear Ireland's preference for Senator Clinton. He singled out Obama in the *Irish
Independent* on May 29, 2008, saying that his tax plans were
a cause of "some worry" to Ireland. Given what both candidates were saying, to the extent he needed to be concerned, he
should have been concerned with both.

O'Dowd also didn't mention that Senator McCain, who
would become the Republican presidential nominee, had
repeatedly called for lowering the US corporate tax rate, which
might also cause problems for Ireland. On June 10, 2008, in a
speech before the National Small Business Summit, McCain
said, "If you give American corporations the highest tax rates
or the second highest tax rates in the world, they're going to go
someplace where they're lower. We need to lower that tax rate.
We need to imitate our friends, the Irish, as a matter of fact."

The strength of the business lobby in the US and the
division between Republicans and Democrats on broad tax
policy caused little to happen. US laws didn't change during
the Obama administration. The first sense that some change
might be on the horizon came in 2016 when President Obama
blocked an inversion of Pfizer into Ireland. An inversion occurs
when a large company buys or merges with a much smaller one
and calls the more tax-favorable foreign country, i.e., Ireland,
its home. In fairness to Pfizer, the company had long had a
presence in Ireland and employed many there, as opposed to
the companies that were solely interested in Ireland for tax
reasons. (Full disclosure: Pfizer is a sponsor of the Mitchell
Scholarship program.)

Candidates Hillary Clinton and Donald Trump talked
tough on jobs overseas. As Fintan O'Toole wrote in the *Irish
Times* in April 2016, "when it became more and more obvious
that tax avoidance was an alluring aspect of Ireland's charms,
we could rely on three things to protect us. First, who didn't love
Ireland? We were a little throwback country where everybody's

ancestors came from. Second, the vast majority of Americans knew as much about corporate tax avoidance as they knew about hurling, so it wasn't a political issue. And third, corporate power was largely unchallenged—both Democrats and Republicans did what the giant corporations wanted, even if that was against the interests of their own voters." Dropping the US corporate tax rate was a priority for President Trump, and in late 2017, he succeeded in getting the US corporate tax rate reduced to 21 percent.

In 2017, a new threat loomed post-Brexit as Conservative prime minister Theresa May announced that Britain's corporate tax rate would fall to 17 percent by 2020.

Irish history has been strong on flight. To resolve our problems we need to stay grounded. This is not to deny that some emigration is good and that much of it is inevitable. . . . Irish emigration has always been a substitute for change and reform.

—Cathal Guiomard, *The Irish Disease and How to Cure It*

When immigration works, ethnicity drops from the foreground to the background over time. It stops being a public destiny and starts being a private source of meaning.

—David Brooks, *New York Times*

Chapter 3

IMMIGRATION MISINFORMATION

In March 2007, I stood in the back of a hotel ballroom on Capitol Hill, surprised and uncomfortable by what I was observing. For some time, Niall O'Dowd had been trying to convince me about his latest cause—obtaining permanent, legal status for Irish people living illegally in the US. He urged me to attend the Irish Lobby for Immigration Reform (ILIR) rally on Capitol Hill. Various politicians paraded in and out to state their support for immigration reform, but it was what went on between speakers, when the politicians were not in the room, that was disturbing. In a crowd sporting tee shirts emblazoned with "Legalize the Irish," a band entertaining the crowd kept mocking a Mexican accent as they repeatedly chanted, "We speak English." When I first heard it, I thought it was one of those moments where something happens at an event that the organizers haven't seen coming, wouldn't approve of, and would quickly bring to a halt. But they didn't, and this went on throughout the rally. The young Irish diplomat standing beside me seemed equally uncomfortable.

That day solidified my views and would ultimately result in my writing an opinion piece on the subject in the *Irish Times* later that year. It was a piece that would enrage O'Dowd and his brother-in-law and colleague in the ILIR, Ciaran Staunton. Since that time, the pair has frequently attacked me, the Mitchell Scholarship program, and the US-Ireland Alliance to an irrational and vindictive degree.

I support legal immigration. Waves of people seeking a better life have been instrumental in the development of the United States, and most of us are the descendants of immigrants. I am also in favor of immigration reform that would create a legal path to citizenship for the vast majority of those now illegally in the US.

But equally, every nation needs to have a sensible immigration policy. September 11, 2001 completely changed the world as Americans knew it, and guarding against letting people in who would do our country harm is a necessary priority. It is also not tenable, nor is it reasonable, to effectively say that if you are in the US illegally, after a while, you'll just get to stay. Ireland doesn't have such a policy, and it shouldn't expect that of the US.

The deportation of those illegally here now is logistically unrealistic, and it simply isn't going to happen. We should pass legislation that creates the path to citizenship but also draws a line under this issue once and for all, and we must refuse to replay this scenario every ten years. We must have a coherent, reasonable, and consistent system whereby people apply from their countries of citizenship and wait their turn—the exception being asylum seekers whose lives are under threat and should receive preference and quick action.

Where I parted company with O'Dowd and the ILIR was in their efforts to create a "special deal" for just the Irish.

Los Angeles Times writer Gregory Rodriguez referred to the "Legalize the Irish" tee shirt phrase as an "in-your-face slogan." It is counterproductive, morally indefensible, and just not politically smart to create such unnecessary tension with Latinos.

O'Dowd had been annoying members of the immigration reform community a full year before that ILIR event I attended in Washington. In a *New York Times* article in March 2006, journalist Nina Bernstein wrote, "Both opponents and supporters of legalization take a more jaundiced view of the Irish role in the debate." It was noticed that the Irish were going off on their own, and race and discrimination permeated the article. O'Dowd's comment, "It's not about being fair, it's about being good," did not go down well with several members of Congress—including Senator John McCain—who distanced themselves by making clear that they were not for special deals. In the October/November 2007 issue of *Magill Magazine*, O'Dowd said, "I'll use whatever tactics I can." On May 5, 2008, Sarah Garland, in a *New York Sun* article, "Immigrants Riled by Irish Push for Special Status," wrote, "An effort by the Irish to secure a special immigration deal solely for illegal immigrants from Ireland isn't sitting well with some of their former partners in the fight for an overhaul of federal immigration policy."

It would be wrong for the US government to usher to the front of the line a subset of those illegally in the US because of skin color. I would love to see more Irish immigrants come to the US, but divide and conquer is not the right strategy. And politically, it won't happen. I wrote my opinion piece a decade ago, when the ILIR was misleading people, and perhaps themselves, that a special deal was just around the corner. It never was. American politicians aren't going to irritate millions of Latinos by giving a special deal to a few thousand Irish. As President Bill Clinton said when he spoke about identity politics to Loyola Marymount graduating seniors in 2016, "Are we going to expand the definition of us and shrink the definition of them? Or shall we just hunker down in the face of uncomfortable realities and just stick with our own crowd? It will be a bleaker future if you do that."

In April 2014, Nancy Pelosi, the then-former Speaker of the House of Representatives, referenced racism as a reason why Republicans were not dealing with immigration. A *Sunday Business Post* piece by Niall Stanage quoted Pelosi as saying, "I think race has something to do with the fact that they're not bringing up an immigration bill. I've heard them say to the Irish: If it were just you, this would be easy." In the fall of 2015, when Stella O'Leary spoke at the Clinton Institute for American Studies at University College Dublin, she claimed that if Irish American Republicans would stick with the Irish American Democrats, "we would probably have a special bill for the Irish at this point." Immigration fixes for just the Irish illegally in the US would be racist.

It is also worth noting that in that hotel ballroom in 2007, I surveyed a room that was largely filled with twenty- to thirty-year-olds. These young people came to the US and overstayed their visas at a time when the Irish economy was booming and they could get jobs at home. They weren't refugees fleeing war-torn countries, poverty, or female genital mutilation in an African country. In fact, Irish government ministers visiting the United States were appealing to the Irish to return home where they were needed to fill jobs.

By the end of the summer of 2006, O'Dowd was hoping to convince Senator Kennedy to push for a special deal for the Irish if broad immigration reform failed to be enacted. That was something Kennedy did not support. How little the Irish are influencing the immigration debate could be seen in "Last Best Chance," an episode of the HBO documentary series *How Democracy Works Now*. The filmmakers shadowed Senators

Kennedy and McCain as they worked on immigration reform. The senators, their staffers, and immigration leaders are constantly seen strategizing, but the Irish were never at the table, or even mentioned.

O'Dowd's pitch at the time was that the Australians had received a special deal. But that deal had nothing to do with anyone illegally in the US. In 2005, President George W. Bush signed a law, resulting from the Australia-United States Free Trade Agreement, which annually provided 10,500 E-3 visas for people with "specialized" skills. They are two-year visas that can be renewed indefinitely. Applicants must have a university degree and a job offer. O'Dowd and company were never seeking something similar to Australia—they wanted permanent status for those already illegally in the US. His arguments about precedent were misleading.

Shortly after I wrote my opinion piece in November 2007, Michael Chertoff, President Bush's secretary of homeland security, was interviewed by Myles Duggan on the *Pat Kenny Show* on RTE. Duggan asked, "There are relatively few Irish illegals as opposed to Latino. . . . Any chance of a separate deal or is it all for one, one for all?" Chertoff responded, "I don't think we could, in good conscience, start to pick people from particular ethnic groups and say, 'Well, this group is going to get treated differently than some other group.' I mean that would lay us open to charges of prejudice and ethnic bias which are unacceptable."

When O'Dowd couldn't argue with the facts of my opinion piece, he opted instead to go after me personally. He never mentioned that he had been on the board of our nonprofit organization and had been supportive, effusively so, for years. And in going after me, he swung wildly. In my piece, I wrote, "There is also talk of trying to mask a 'special deal' by cloaking it in innocuous immigration provisions but this is just an attempt to, as they say on Wall Street, 'put lipstick on that pig.'"

It is clear that my reference was about legislative strategy, but O'Dowd absurdly suggested that I was calling Irish people pigs. He hopes that if he keeps repeating false assertions, they might stick with people who can't be bothered to investigate. (Disregard for the truth did not originate with the 2016 election.) The phrase "lipstick on a pig" is commonly used, and just months later, candidate Obama would use it, and the year before, John McCain used it in talking about a different policy proposal.

The exact number of Irish illegally in the US is unknown, but neither immigration experts nor successive Irish ambassadors to the US believed the number to be the 50,000 or more as often claimed. One Irish immigration expert told me that, estimated on a number of good sources, he believed the 50,000 to be exaggerated by a factor of between five and ten.

O'Dowd came up with his number of 50,000 by taking the rates of Irish emigrating to the US in previous decades and extrapolating to suggest that the same number came every year through the 1990s and 2000s. But that didn't take into account that, not only were the Irish not coming during the boom; many returned to a prosperous Ireland. Adrian Flannelly, chairman of the Irish Radio Network in New York, told Nina Bernstein of the *New York Times* in November 2004, "It's the complete reversal of the American dream." Bernstein wrote that "Christina McElwaine, a spokeswoman for the Irish Consulate in New York, said the reversal seems unprecedented in scale. In 2002, after several years of strong economic growth and declining emigration, Ireland's census recorded 26,000 more Irish who returned than left."

In July 2006, Cox News Service quoted O'Dowd as saying that the ILIR was "formed last year in response to the growing struggles of Irish illegal immigrants in the United States, which he estimates number 50,000 to 60,000." But just seven months earlier, O'Dowd's wife and the editor of the *Irish*

Voice, Debbie McGoldrick, wrote, "The new lobby group created by the *Irish Voice* . . . will advocate on behalf of the estimated 20,000–30,000 Irish undocumented in the US." Are we to believe that in the space of seven months, at the height of Ireland's economic boom, the number doubled?

Boston Globe journalist Kevin Cullen wrote of the reverse exodus in the *New York Times* on March 22, 2007: "The Irish government estimates that, worldwide, about 150,000 Irish-born people have moved back to Ireland since 2001. . . . US Census figures document the American exodus: There were 160,000 Irish-born living in the US in 2000; since then the total has dropped by 20 percent, to an estimated 128,000." In June 2008, Ireland's minister of state for integration policy, Conor Lenihan, told the *Wall Street Journal* that "half a million of our own people came home as part of the early years of the boom."

The Migration Policy Institute, an independent, nonpartisan, Washington, DC, think tank that analyzes the movement of people worldwide, looks at "unauthorized" immigrants by country. Not seeing a reference to Ireland, I wrote to inquire about this in November 2016. Michelle Mittelstadt, director of communications, told me, "The numbers coming from Europe are too small to be disaggregated by country of origin." The Institute looks at sample sizes used by the US Census Bureau. Mittelstadt went on, "The most we can say is this: Ireland is not among the top 50 countries. The smallest population among the top 50 is 16,000 unauthorized immigrants. Therefore, the Irish population will be less than 16,000. By how much, we cannot tell you."

Some Irish political leaders have not helped the situation with their unwillingness to be frank about the futility of their efforts to obtain a special deal. They know what the score is from their conversations with US politicians, but they sugarcoat things so as not to be seen as the bearers of bad news back home. And they can be hypocritical in the process. In

September 2007, in the very week that Irish foreign minister Dermot Ahern was in the US arguing for a special deal for the Irish, Ireland's justice minister, Brian Lenihan, said there would be no amnesty for illegals in Ireland: "Amnesty or regularisation, in my view, undermines the system of legal migration. They can exacerbate the problem of illegal migration by sending out the wrong message and give rise to a belief that further amnesties will become available in the future."

Irish government ministers have spent too much limited capital in the US on this issue. It also amounts to sanctioning something they should not. The American embassy in Dublin does not advocate for Americans who may be illegally in Ireland. As some Irish commentators have suggested, such tacit support may be the result of Irish governments' own failings. As Cathal Guiomard wrote in his 1995 book, *The Irish Disease and How to Cure It*, "Irish emigration has always been a substitute for change and reform." Guilt may drive some Irish politicians who realize emigration serves to lessen the economic burdens at home.

I received more emails related to my opinion piece than for any other I've ever written. The general theme was "Good for you for saying that; about time someone did." Among those who welcomed the piece were many people from Ireland and the US, including the former CEO of Coca-Cola, Don Keough; Adare Manor owner Tom Kane; the man behind the growth of Silicon Valley, Tom McEnery; Garda commissioner Pat Byrne; author Peter Quinn; immigration activist and Steve Jobs's wife, Laurene Powell-Jobs; University College Cork immigration expert Piaras MacEinri; and former taoiseach Garret FitzGerald. Senator David Norris, never one to shrink from taking a public stance, went on the record in the Oireachtas in support. Republican US congressman Peter King, whom O'Dowd was at odds with over immigration, joked with me that he was happy that I was now in O'Dowd's crosshairs instead of him. Cecilia Muñoz, then the head of the National Council of La Raza, and later President Obama's point person on immigration, thanked me, writing, "We can all be in the struggle for legalization together."

For all the whinging of the ILIR, Ireland actually does very well. According to 2008 Department of Homeland Security data on temporary visas for workers and families, of 192 countries, only 20 received more visas than Ireland. Given the country's small population, that is incredible. In raw numbers alone, Ireland received more than Sweden, Taiwan, South Africa, Turkey, Denmark, Belgium, Norway, Chile, New Zealand, Singapore, and Poland.

Ireland received 14,736 such visas. Jamaica is the country next above Ireland, but if you take away the large number of their visas that are seasonal and agricultural, Ireland received more. Next, with more visas than Ireland, is the Netherlands, but that country's population was more than three times that of Ireland so, proportionate to population, Ireland did better. Next was Spain with 21,850 visas. Spain's population was 47 million. You get the picture. Only Israel and Mexico did as well as Ireland. Mexico received more visas that year than any other country: 360,903. If you deduct the seasonal workers, many agricultural, Mexico's total would have been 122,270. But even if you take the higher number and consider Mexico had a population of 108 million, Mexico only did slightly better than Ireland in terms of proportion to population.

As Ireland became wealthier, fewer Irish chose to move to the US. While more than 17,000 Irish immigrated to the US in 1994 alone—just before the Irish economy began to boom—the number of Irish immigrants in any given year since 1996 has never exceeded 1,600. This decrease in immigration is of concern in that it causes a significant reduction in the number of people who can educate Americans about contemporary Ireland. But relying on immigration to sustain ties is head-in-sand thinking. We should not hope for economic disaster in Ireland to get more immigrants.

In the 2008 campaign, just as O'Dowd falsely suggested that Hillary Clinton would be better for Ireland when it came to American multinationals and tax, he did the same on immigration. But again, there was virtually no daylight between Clinton, Obama, and McCain on the issue. All were for comprehensive immigration reform, and none were for a special deal for the Irish.

On October 30, 2007, in a Democratic primary debate in Philadelphia, NBC moderator Tim Russert pointed out that New York governor Eliot Spitzer proposed giving driver's licenses to illegal immigrants. Russert noted that Clinton told the *Nashua, New Hampshire* editorial board that Spitzer's plan "makes a lot of sense." Russert asked her, "Why does it make a lot of sense?" Clinton didn't deny that was her view, and her answer again suggested she supported Spitzer's plan. Fellow candidate Senator Chris Dodd chimed in and said he found that "troublesome," that driving was a privilege. Clinton flip-flopped on the spot by interrupting with, "I just want to add I did not say that it should be done, but I certainly recognize why Governor Spitzer is trying to do it." Her fellow candidates were incredulous. Russert challenged her. Obama said he was confused by her answer: "I can't tell whether she was for it or against it." Obama was unequivocal and said he favored granting licenses to illegal immigrants. Given O'Dowd's agenda, Obama gave the right answer. But O'Dowd stayed quiet. Had the roles been reversed, O'Dowd's *Irish Voice* would have trumpeted Clinton's support for driver's licenses, but I don't recall him complaining about her stance, or praising Obama for his. Again, the facts were not going to get in the way of O'Dowd's narrative of Clinton.

O'Dowd is a huge supporter of Clinton, yet she never suggested she supports a special deal. Her stance on a special deal is no different than mine, but O'Dowd attacks me and raised money for her.

In Washington in March 2008, a few months after my piece appeared in the *Irish Times*, Irish prime minister Bertie Ahern finally frankly called it as it was, saying that a special deal for the Irish was "not on." In that article by Mark Hennessy, the Irish illegally in the US were said to be "between 3,000 and 20,000." It's unclear if that number came from Ahern or the *Irish Times*, but it does suggest that at least someone was unwilling to accept O'Dowd's unsubstantiated claims of 50,000. O'Dowd called Ahern's remarks "totally misinformed." For good measure, O'Dowd "questioned whether Ahern had any real 'clout' in the US or was just engaged in 'airy-fairy' exchanges with US leaders on St. Patrick's Day." O'Dowd again misled by trying to suggest that what he was seeking wasn't an amnesty, and he suggested that Mexico was working on a similar deal. That is absurd on the face of it. If the majority of illegal immigrants were Mexican, why would Mexico argue for a deal to keep the remaining handful out?

In February, when O'Dowd wrote that Mexican president Felipe Calderón "announced that he was seeking a bilateral treaty for his countrymen in America with the US government," I called the Mexican embassy and spoke with the diplomat who dealt with the immigration issue. He told me that Mexico was not seeking any bilateral deal on immigration. Rather, President Calderón was seeking a bilateral deal on security issues concerning drug trafficking and crime.

In defense of his proposition for an Irish amnesty, O'Dowd regularly said that many countries have reached, or are pursuing, their own bilateral arrangements with the United States. In addition to the inaccurate suggestions about Mexico and Australia, El Salvador was given as an example. The insinuation is that such bilateral agreements relate directly to the problem of illegal immigrants. Untrue. There were no special deals for illegal immigrants, and any argument that seeks to establish a precedent for an Irish deal based on these "deals" is groundless. The fact that such a deceptive line of argument went unchecked is indicative of the lack of scrutiny that O'Dowd's claims have received.

And when O'Dowd realized there would be no special deal, he, incredibly, started to claim that he had never sought a special deal. Marian Finucane was one of the few to challenge him on her RTE radio program on March 22, 2008. O'Dowd told Finucane that the taoiseach was mistaken: "We were not looking for a special deal." Finucane, referring to me, said, "She said you were." O'Dowd: "She probably did but she is also incorrect." The record is overwhelmingly clear. O'Dowd was looking for a special deal. For example, on June 29, 2007, Denis Staunton wrote in the *Irish Times*, "Niall O'Dowd, chairman of the Irish Lobby for Immigration Reform, said he had already discussed with Mr Ahern the possibility of seeking a special deal for Irish immigrants. 'In some ways it's easier because you're not trying to deal with an overwhelming reality for Americans. You're talking about a much smaller number of people,' he said."

While on Finucane's program, O'Dowd also mentioned El Salvador. I spoke with both the political officer at the US embassy in El Salvador and a diplomat at the El Salvador embassy in Washington. Neither knew of any talk of a bilateral deal for illegal Salvadorans. More than two hundred thousand Salvadorans had Temporary Protected Status (TPS), which allowed them to be in the US. This was a humanitarian response to devastating earthquakes in El Salvador a few years earlier. Having that status does not lead to permanent residency. (In January 2018, the Trump administration announced it would end the protected status.)

In May 2008, Brian Cowen became Ireland's new prime minister. About his St. Patrick's Day visit to the US in March 2009, Marion McKeone wrote in the *Sunday Tribune*, "There was also precious little progress on the issue of undocumented Irish workers in the US—aside from a tacit acceptance by the Irish government that the prospect of any special deal for undocumented Irish is dead in the water. Instead of trying to find a solution for the thousands of Irish currently working illegally, the Irish government will focus on pushing a new bilateral deal that would allow thousands of Irish citizens to receive renewable two-year work visas for the US." This new kind of visa, which no one had been seeking, was a bit of a bait and switch.

Meanwhile, Irish foreign minister Micheál Martin warned Irish citizens who were thinking of working illegally in the US to rethink their plans. McKeone was prescient when she wrote, "Given the scale and complexity of the domestic and foreign policy crises Obama is currently grappling with, comprehensive immigration reform is not something the US president is likely to tackle any time soon. During the meeting with Cowen, he noted it was something he 'would like to get around to,' but the truth is that nobody within his own party wants him to grapple with such a potentially explosive issue in his first term. Even assuming he secures a second term, any attempt to tackle this problem is unlikely to come much before 2014."

It would be an understatement to say that O'Dowd and Staunton have been on the warpath since I wrote my opinion piece. In 2010, when the Oireachtas was debating legislation to provide funding for the George J. Mitchell Scholarship program, the pair pulled out all the stops trying to prevent passage. The email sent to members of the Oireachtas gives a sense of their vitriol. (It is also an example of irrational behavior. As O'Dowd hates Oxford, he should support a scholarship that has future American leaders going to Ireland instead. But in his obsession with attacking me, he would happily throw out the baby with the bath water.) This is the email that Ciaran Staunton, Niall O'Dowd's brother-in-law, sent around:

Subject: Fw: Irish Taxpayers money should not be financing
Trina Vargo: Niall O Dowd

US-Ireland Alliance
Should Be De-funded

Who is Trina Vargo, who heads the US-Ireland Alliance?
She is the woman who wrote an op-ed piece for the Irish
Times last year proclaiming that trying to help young Irish
undocumented was akin to "putting lipstick on a pig."

Welcome to a new generation of leadership, a
writer of Unionist background who slams Irish American
organizations at every opportunity, and a Portuguese
American who compares Irish to pigs and heads an
organization that about 99% of Irish Americans have never
heard of.

That would be Trina Vargo, head of the US-Ireland
Alliance which sends a dozen or so well-heeled American
students to Ireland every year on a rip-off of the Rhodes
Scholar program, and gets millions from Ireland, Britain
and the US government for doing so. Vargo, a Portuguese
American with little Irish heritage, latched on to the issue
when she worked with Senator Edward Kennedy.

Even before Stanage's article ran, Vargo sent out an
email to every politician in Ireland highlighting the piece,
proclaiming that the old leadership in Irish America was
over and she alone represented the new leadership.

What is the US-Ireland Alliance? In addition to the
government funding it receives, it is also funded by private
sources—mainly the property speculators in Ireland who
have brought the country to the brink of ruin.

Back in Ireland the alliance continues to take funds
from the Irish government, despite the horrific recession
that has left the country on its knees. If you ask Irish people

they would be sure to say that funding American students to come to Ireland is not their priority right now.

Irish Americans will mobilize here and end the funding from America for this group that now purports to treat us like idiots and as completely out of touch.

The Irish government should re-prioritize too and tell the US-Ireland Alliance enough is enough, and spend taxpayer money on better issues. Maybe then the message will get through to the likes of Unionist tradition Stanage and "lipstick on a pig" Vargo that Irish Americans are not so easily duped and misled.

US-Ireland Alliance
Should Be De-funded

Niall O Dowd

The Staunton/O'Dowd email also refers to Irish journalist Niall Stanage, who wrote a book about the Obama campaign entitled *Redemption Song*. His great sin was having painted an accurate picture of Irish America, one that goes against the image that O'Dowd portrays, and because Stanage praised the work of the US-Ireland Alliance in the process, he also is persona non grata. The suggestion is that neither of us is sufficiently Irish. Stanage is from a Protestant background in Northern Ireland and studied at Oxford. O'Dowd regularly spews the word "Oxford" in a way meant to suggest that anyone who would attend Oxford must be a Unionist. (He seems to forget that President Clinton attended Oxford, as did Martin Mansergh, who also played an important role in the peace process.)

The underlying racism also is evident in the reference to me as Portuguese. While I would be happy to have some Portuguese ancestry in the mix, the fact is that there is none. I can only assume that was meant to suggest I am a Latina

American. Again, I'm not. O'Dowd knows that I'm partially of Irish American descent, and he named me one of his "Top 100 Irish Americans" for several years in his magazine (obviously before I wrote the opinion piece). O'Dowd and Staunton define Irishness to suit themselves. If you agree with them, you're Irish; if you don't, you're not. Most of the diaspora is a mix of several ethnicities. Maybe we should all take blood tests to see if we're Irish enough?

On January 5, 2008, I happened to be home with CNN on the television in the background when I heard someone screaming at Mitt Romney at an "Ask Mitt Anything" town hall meeting at the Pinkerton Academy High School in Derry, New Hampshire. It was Ciaran Staunton sounding quite unhinged. He wasn't politely challenging but ranting, "Have you no shame." The Republican candidate for president was perfectly civil and said, "We simply cannot take all the people in the world who want to come to America. . . . We're going to enforce the law. . . . I love legal immigration, but I want to end illegal immigration." Staunton was booed and shouted down by the rest of the audience, but his behavior was so extreme that it garnered national attention, including a *New York Daily News* headline, "Queen's Bar Owner Assails Mitt Romney Over Immigration Flip-Flop."

In that previously referenced 2015 UCD interview with Stella O'Leary, Conor O'Clery asked why she was support-ing Hillary Clinton rather than Irishman Martin O'Malley, who was also running for president. O'Leary said, "A friend of Ireland is not necessarily someone with an Irish name." She went on to say, "O'Malley is Irish on his father's side, his mother is German." She seemed to be grasping to suggest he was therefore somehow *less* Irish.

The O'Dowd/Staunton email was rife with other errors. Members of the Irish Parliament saw the personal attacks for what they were, and the email negativity backfired. During the debate about the Mitchell Scholarship funding, one member of the Seanad, Senator Ned O'Sullivan, stated in the chamber that "I was disappointed by an e-mail I received before I entered the Chamber. . . . It was from a fairly notable Irish American who seemed to be casting aspersions on some of the people involved in the scholarship's administration in the US. This is a red herring, as the important issue is the scholarship's value."

Both houses of the Irish Parliament supported the legislation to provide matching funding for the Mitchell Scholarship program by unanimous consent. No party objected. The only member of the Oireachtas who objected, after the fact, was Fine Gael TD Michael Ring. However, he did not speak against the bill when it was before the Parliament. His own party supported the bill, its education spokesperson spoke in favor of the bill, and the party's education platform cited the Mitchell Scholarship program as the template for how a Fine Gael government would extend this program to other countries.

O'Dowd, who had served nearly ten years on our advisory board, had nothing but positive things to say about the organization and me in an *Irish Voice* article published on December 17, 2003:

> There has not been a more dynamic start-up of an Irish organization since the American Ireland Fund. . . . The Mitchell program has been an unqualified success, thanks in large measure to Vargo's extraordinary ability to access funding, convince skeptics the idea can work and her unbridled enthusiasm for placing Ireland on the American academic map.

But O'Dowd and Staunton never let it go. All this vehemence over one accurate opinion piece in 2007.

The only thing that has changed about the Mitchell since he wrote that praise is that it has become more popular and prestigious, and now there are more than two hundred Mitchell Scholars, across the US and the world, who are great ambassadors for Ireland. One serves as a San Francisco supervisor, another is in the Massachusetts House of Representatives, and another has been so innovative with a homeless shelter in Arkansas that her work was replicated across the US. One is working on research to combat malaria, another to combat climate change. Several are authors. Others are doctors and researchers. Two have been legal counsels for the US Trade Representative and the Department of Commerce. Several have worked in the US Department of State.

The Mitchells are also building future ties between the US and Ireland. Nick Johnson, a tenured assistant professor at Trinity College Dublin, is an expert on Samuel Beckett. From 2015 to 2016, he was involved with two Beckett world premieres, working as dramaturg for Pan Pan's *Cascando* in Dublin, and as director for *No's Knife* at Lincoln Center in New York. Nick is a constant bridge between the US and Ireland.

Kelly Kirkpatrick now resides in Cork, where she served as the director of operations for Sean O'Sullivan's venture capital firm SOSV. Kelly started the Mathletes Challenge (which later became LearnStorm Ireland), partnering with Ireland's Department of Education and the US-based nonprofit Khan Academy to pilot a new math competition for students in Ireland. In just three years, LearnStorm grew to 160,000 students in four global regions.

Jasmin Weaver worked for several years as the deputy director of the Office of Intergovernmental Relations for the city of Seattle, Washington. She coordinated and facilitated the interactions of city representatives, such as the mayor and city council members, with other governments, including Ireland.

When Pulitzer Prize– and National Book Award–winner Tim Egan launched his book about Thomas Francis Meagher, *The Immortal Irishman*, Jasmin was asked to introduce him before an audience of hundreds. Jasmin's husband, Noah Purcell, obtained an MA at UCD when Jasmin was a student there. He is now the Solicitor General for Washington State (he blocked President Trump's travel ban). He was also a Supreme Court clerk—perhaps the only person with an Irish university degree to hold that distinction, until Alec Schierenbeck became the first Mitchell Scholar Supreme Court clerk, for Justice Breyer during the 2018 Court term.

Winnie M. Li is pursuing a PhD in Media and Communications at the London School of Economics. She is looking at the impact of digital media on the public dialogue about rape and sexual assault. Winnie was the victim of a violent assault and rape in Belfast in 2008. Her novel about this, *Dark Chapter*, was critically acclaimed. She has spoken on the topic many times in Ireland and Northern Ireland.

The issue of the Irish illegally in the US came up yet again during St. Patrick's Day meetings in March 2018.

On March 15, Suzanne Lynch reported in the *Irish Times* that the Irish delegation was now talking about the numbers of "undocumented" being 10,000. John Deasy, the government's envoy to the US Congress, reportedly came up with the idea of a swap, which was expressed by the taoiseach in his meeting with President Trump. Americans would be given more work visas and there would be "protections" for American citizens who want to retire to Ireland, in exchange for "protection" for the Irish illegally in the US. Deasy reported that "we reached agreement to pursue a bilateral deal and that's real progress."

Credit is due to Deasy for at least stating the numbers as they more likely are (around 10,000). But the Congress was never going to support any special deal for the Irish illegally in the US. Ultimately, the Irish government tried to get the unused Australian E3 visas (for professionals to come from Ireland legally), but even that failed at the end of 2018 when a Republican senator from Arkansas, Tom Cotton, prevented passage.

I wouldn't underestimate the lack of enthusiasm with US politicians for what would even appear to be a special deal for the Irish. I just don't see politicians annoying millions of Latinos to put to the front of the line maybe 10,000 Irish. I still believe the Irish will only be sorted as part of a comprehensive plan and if, by some chance, some sort of special deal was ever arranged, it could create a bigger problem for Ireland years down the road with a dominant constituency that would not likely forget that the Irish were for themselves alone.

Elected officials have only limited control over what their officials do. . . . Bureaucracies have their own private agenda, involving increased power, size and perks.

—Cathal Guiomard, *The Irish Disease and How to Cure It*

Under the umbrella of the state . . . monopolies and near monopolies . . . forgive each other their many failings so that they could all continue to lead a quiet life. This is a certain recipe for mediocrity and corruption, and in Ireland we see both . . . lumbered with an institutional framework in which rewards are not based on merit. . . . By separating rewards from productive effort, initiative is discouraged, talent is wasted and mediocrity slinks into the breach.

—Cathal Guiomard, *The Irish Disease and How to Cure It*

You're right, those certificates are nonsense. I so admire you. You have guts. But you know, we can't always tell the truth.

—A former executive of Enterprise Ireland

Cordelia! mend your speech a little, Lest it may mar your fortunes.

—Shakespeare, *King Lear*

Chapter 4

BUREAUCRATS

The slow pace of change in the US-Ireland relationship cannot be blamed on ignorance. Many in Irish and Northern Ireland political and diplomatic circles were aware of the shift; they just continued to ignore it for years, and that continues to some degree. The unwillingness and inability to turn the ship around more quickly can be attributed to bureaucratic inertia but also to a culture that includes a resistance to frank analysis.

While a large amount of the blame for Ireland's dramatic economic fall has justifiably been laid at the doorstep of bankers, regulators, and politicians, my experiences suggest that bureaucrats are a large part of Ireland's problems. While the majority of the civil service is competent and conscientious, a substantial minority has an unhealthy impact on the country.

I haven't seen a lot written about the Irish psyche. In the 2006 Martin Scorsese film, *The Departed*, screenwriter Bill Monahan included a line that is attributed to Sigmund Freud about the Irish being impervious to psychoanalysis. One of the best things I found was a chapter in a book mainly about the

Irish economy. In 1995, Cathal Guiomard, then a professor at University College Dublin, wrote *The Irish Disease and How to Cure It*. When the book was released, the following appeared in the *Irish Times* Quidnunc column:

> New Book Attempts to Shine Blow-Torch of Economic Modernisation up Ireland's Posterior. It's not the kind of language one would associate with a 252-page tome written by a UCD academic on the subject of Ireland's economic ills. *The Irish Disease and How to Cure It* by economics lecturer Cathal Guiomard is published next week. Few national institutions escape condemnation. The Central Bank (for which Mr. Guiomard used to work), the semi-state companies, the Civil Service in general and Department of Finance in particular, the political system, the Irish people generally and even—God help us—some *Irish Times* columnists are variously excoriated for their indolence, defeatism, smugness and complacency.

The book about what was holding the Irish economy back was published just as the economy was heading into a long period of sustained growth. Because of that, I suspect it was given short shrift at the time. But the chapter on Irish behavior remains informative and insightful.

What Guiomard illuminates did not go away with the rise of the Celtic Tiger. If anything, economic success engendered a certain level of bravado, a sometimes seemingly willed confidence that belied an insecurity lurking beneath. Martin McDonagh's play *The Cripple of Inishmaan*, which is set on the Aran Islands off the west coast of Ireland, includes a character named Johnny Pateen Mike, the island village's purveyor of news and gossip. The play, set in the 1930s, is peppered with the character's regular pronouncements of how great Ireland is, such as "and Ireland mustn't be such a bad place so, if the Yanks want to come to Ireland to do their filming." While he utters this with boastful pride, one gets the sense that Johnny Pateen is saying this as much to convince himself as others that Ireland is a great place. After President Obama visited Ireland in 2010, Shane Hegarty wrote in the *Irish Times* that the Irish want "to be told we are great." Economic success and this kind of posturing allowed the underlying psychological issues Guiomard wrote about to be ignored. Yet some of these behaviors contributed to recent problems and, if not more widely and seriously addressed, will continue to hamper Ireland.

I have spent the last twenty-five years of my life extolling all that is positive about Ireland. But blindly "wearing the green jersey" doesn't really do much to contribute to addressing the subterranean problems that must be tackled if Ireland is to fully bounce back and if the US-Ireland relationship is to be sustained.

There are cultural differences that must be understood. One is that Americans more often say what we mean and think, the Irish less so. Hugo Hamilton in *The Speckled People: A Memoir of a Half-Irish Childhood* recounts how his German mother told him, "In Ireland, you can't ask people anything. It's not like Germany where a question is just a question. In Ireland people get offended by questions, because it's a way of saying what you're thinking."

"No" may not be "no." If you offer an American a second helping of food, if he or she wants it, they'll accept on the first offer. And if they decline, they really don't want any more. If you offer an Irish person seconds, their default response is to decline. A Beckettian ritual follows: "Have more." "I can't." "You must." "I can't." It is usually only on about the third offering that the food is accepted. One explanation I was given is that this verbal dance has its roots in the Famine. Being mannerly, an Irish person who may have been down to his or her last crumb would still offer food or drink to their guest. Assuming the host didn't have it to spare, the guest would decline. It was understood that only if the offer was made several times did the host actually have it to give.

This level of indirectness can cause misunderstandings in business settings as well. When Irish delegations met with Senator Kennedy, I regularly advised them beforehand to quickly get to the point with him, as his schedule was arranged in fifteen-minute increments. This was disorienting to the Irish, who often have a cup of tea and a meandering, half-hour warm-up conversation.

I recall one meeting I had with Noel Dempsey, Ireland's then minister for education. He asked to see me about something having to do with the Mitchell Scholarship program. It was one of those long, circuitous conversations, and I was trying to figure out why I was there. A half hour into the conversation, it still wasn't clear to me. It wasn't until I was walking out the door that Dempsey casually dropped one sentence, and I knew that was the entire point of the meeting. It is only from years of experience that I didn't miss what was made to sound like an afterthought as I was leaving. In fact, it was the lead, buried. During the peace process, I often had to identify for my American colleagues in Congress the operative sentence in Sinn Fein/IRA statements. It was rarely in the first paragraph; it had to be excavated.

The aforementioned examples are common and harmless, but there is a fine line between this lack of directness and the more sinister. From an American perspective, Irish people simply lie more often. Acclaimed film director Jim Sheridan told me that the habit of lying has roots in the early part of the twentieth century, when it was necessary for the Irish to lie to the British occupiers. The habit has been passed down as a cultural memory. While each culture has its own idiosyncrasies, many of which are endearing, the unusually high level of evasiveness and outright lying has been at the heart of many of Ireland's current problems. Irish poet Eavan Boland said, "We learn to evade the truth in small countries with powerful histories by decorating it."

Cathal Guiomard wrote of "victim Irishness," the recurring themes of which he defined as "negativity and defeatism, migration and mediocrity." What he wrote twenty years ago, before the boom, was prescient and could have been written after Ireland's more recent economic collapse: "Helplessness: refusing to accept our share of responsibility for our present predicament, we see ourselves as victims of foreign aggression in the past, foreign multinationals today and, no doubt, a 'foreign' European super-state in the future. . . . Peripherality is as much a state of mind as a fact of geography." How many times, after the 2008 economic crash, did Taoiseach Brian Cowen blame Lehman Brothers for Ireland's problems and Irish people blame the Troika?

Some in Ireland, particularly in the political realm, frequently confuse criticism with not being a friend of Ireland. Such accusations were regularly leveled against those who predicted the economy was in for a crash landing. The Fianna Fail government, as well as the wealthy, thought that if one didn't talk about problems, there were none. As if talking down the economy were something that could actually be done.

In 2009, *New York Times* Nobel Prize–winning columnist Paul Krugman wrote a piece entitled "Erin Go Broke," in which he opposed the Irish government's bailout of the banks. Ireland's then tanaiste Mary Coughlan called Krugman's article "neither helpful, nor in my view appropriate." She seemed not to recognize that Krugman is an independent columnist expressing a view, not an Irish government spokesperson.

There is a history of this all-or-nothing attitude. You're either with us or against us. Regarding one's views on Northern Ireland, one was, or was not, "sound on the national question." Criticism is often met with a need to find some explanation for why the offender has not fully bought into the orthodoxy. They must be a Protestant, a West Brit, or Dublin 4, a reference to the postal code of the city's tonier neighborhood. Dermot Gallagher, Ireland's one-time ambassador to the US, thought it amusing to introduce me to Taoiseach Albert Reynolds by saying that my family "took the soup," a reference as explained earlier to Irish who, during the Famine, were given soup by Protestant clergy if they'd convert. My family actually came to the US more than one hundred years before the Famine, but the intro suggested that I was, as someone raised Protestant, suspect.

"Inappropriate" seems to be a word often used for unwelcome criticism. A former German ambassador to Ireland, Christian Pauls, was reprimanded by the Department of Foreign Affairs in 2007 after it was reported in the *Irish Times* that he had "described Ireland as a 'coarse place' where junior ministers earn more than the German Chancellor and 'chaotic' hospital waiting lists were tolerated." Ambassador Gallagher, who was then the secretary general of the Department of Foreign Affairs, complained to the German embassy that the remarks were "inaccurate, misinformed, and inappropriate."

I have regularly listened to the Irish criticize the US. Sometimes I agree. I try not to take it personally. Many Irish criticize but don't like being criticized. As Shane Hegarty wrote in that 2010 *Irish Times* piece, "The Irish can be self-critical yet thin-skinned, sensitive to minor slights, yearning for affirmation." The brilliant abbot of Glenstal Abbey, Mark Patrick Hederman, told Marian Finucane that the "Irish public have been violently opposed to being shown exactly what they look like."

This propensity is even stronger in Northern Ireland. In Senator George Mitchell's book *Making Peace*, he noted that people there are "quick to take offense at real or perceived slights. They have a highly developed sense of grievance."

A common Irish phrase that has already been mentioned is "putting on the green jersey." The expression means that if one is truly a friend of Ireland, one should simply be a cheerleader for the country. One can be positive 90 percent of the time, but some will fixate on the 10 percent of negative comments. I know from experience.

I have always been suspect with some Unionist politicians in Northern Ireland, given my role in securing that visa for Gerry Adams to visit the United States in 1994. This would continue to manifest itself, particularly in the early years of the US-Ireland Alliance, when repeated insinuations were made that the organization was not really a nonpartisan organization. These characterizations were made by David Trimble in a letter to the editor of the *Irish Times*, by Roy Beggs, Sr., in the House of Commons, and by Roy Beggs, Jr., in the Northern Ireland Assembly.

In a 2001 *Belfast Telegraph* article entitled "Anger over Mitchell Bursary Scheme," Beggs, Jr., was quoted as saying, "There is also a question of political balance. The scholarships are run by the US-Ireland Alliance, whose President Trina Vargo was recently quoted in the media standing up for Sinn Fein." Yet the piece he referred to was entitled "Sinn Fein Must Work to Restore US Confidence in Peace Process." As the title suggested, I was heavily critical of Sinn Fein. I also criticized the Ulster Unionist Party for its shortcomings. But it is not enough for Unionists that one criticizes equally. Any criticism of the UUP at all caused one to be branded a Republican sympathizer, a fellow traveler.

David Trimble, former head of the Ulster Unionist Party in Northern Ireland, wrote in the *Washington Post* on the issue of

Sinn Fein being "anti-American" because of their lack of support for the Bush administration on the matter of Iraq. I noted that Americans simply don't care what Sinn Fein thinks about American foreign policy and that by raising such nonissues, Trimble was merely seeking to deflect attention from the real issues of Northern Ireland, issues that he had a responsibility and an opportunity to resolve. In response, Trimble wrote that the US-Ireland Alliance is "supposedly nonpartisan" in another attempt to suggest the organization was Republican, in the Irish sense of the word.

Sinn Fein also does not take well to differences of opinion. Relations cooled considerably in 2005 when I advised Senator Kennedy against meeting with Gerry Adams on St. Patrick's Day because of the reported involvement of IRA members in the murder of Robert McCartney and the Northern Bank robbery in Belfast. Senator Kennedy refused to meet Adams, and President Bush and Senator Hillary Clinton followed suit. When McCartney's sisters came to Washington, Kennedy asked if, since I knew the Hill, I would help the women efficiently navigate the labyrinthine warren of Capitol Hill office buildings. This was noticed by Sinn Fein's Washington representative, Rita O'Hare, who either guessed, or was told, that I was behind Kennedy's snub of Adams. Rita had long worked for Sinn Fein in Washington, and we had always gotten along, but she never spoke to me again after that. For all Sinn Fein's assertions that pressure on them never worked, it did in fact. Progress was made when the US took a hard line on Sinn Fein following 9/11, and decommissioning followed shortly after Kennedy and the others snubbed Adams in 2005.

Not wishing to hear dissent is not the sole domain of any party. Fine Gael came to power in 2010, and the new foreign minister and tanaiste, Eamon Gilmore, in disagreeing with my view that the International Fund for Ireland (IFI/explained later) had served its purpose, told me that my publicly stated views on the matter amounted to lobbying against the interests of the Irish government and Northern Ireland, and that therefore damage was being done to the relationship.

In an August 2013 piece in the *Irish Times*, Dan Keenan reported that, as far back as 1989, there were concerns about what IFI money was being spent on. Congressman Brian Donnelly visited Ireland in January 1989 and warned Taoiseach Charles Haughey and Tanaiste Brian Lenihan of a "possible erosion of support in the US Congress for future contributions to the fund." Donnelly specifically raised concerns about money spent on a betting establishment, refurbishing a bank branch, a visitor center at the Bushmills whiskey distillery, and "a grant of more than IR£1 million for a fisheries research vessel for the British government." The Irish response was to tell Donnelly that support in the US could erode if Donnelly criticized it. A cable from the US embassy in Dublin back to the State Department reported Lenihan "warned that too much public criticism could become a self-fulfilling prophesy." This was not unlike what Gilmore would say to me years later.

In March 2011, the Irish economy was in tatters. Elections had just been held, Fianna Fail was decimated, and Fine Gael would lead the next government. Young people in Ireland were voting with their feet. With few jobs at home, many were leaving for places where the jobs were, like Australia and Canada. There could have been a silver lining to the crash, but in 2017, real reform seemed scant.

By "bureaucrats," I refer to a state of mind. There are bureaucrats who aren't bureaucratic, and non-bureaucrats who behave like bureaucrats. For me, these are people who tend to do little more than punch a clock, protect their turf, and avoid failure by taking no initiative and, worse, attempt to block anyone who does.

Competitiveness Reports are published annually by the World Economic Forum, the group behind Davos. In the

2013–2014 report, when it came to the most problematic factors for doing business in Ireland, "inefficient government bureaucracy" was second only to "access to financing."

While some Americans may be overly patriotic, many Irish are not patriotic enough. I rarely hear Irish bureaucrats talk about what is good for their country as the reason they are in their jobs or as a motivating factor.

By patriotism I don't mean the "aren't we the greatest country on earth" American variety that many of my Irish friends tend to mock, often fairly. I mean the feeling of wanting to do something for community, country, and the world—for a cause greater than oneself. While I see it in some, I don't see it as commonly as I do in the United States. In Ireland, many bureaucrats have a sense of entitlement. One phrase used in the Department of Foreign Affairs about the desirability of becoming an ambassador is that it comes with a car and a cook.

At the highest levels of the bureaucracy in Ireland is a permanent class. The US system includes a lot of political appointees. While that can be negative, in some ways, changes of administrations in the US result in a lot of officials being swept out as the new crowd comes in. Not all political appointees are good, but their agenda is the president's. In Ireland, many senior officials see ministers as mere nuisances who fortunately won't be in the position long enough to alter the agendas of the unelected.

Ireland's late taoiseach Garret FitzGerald was a man of great integrity, and he was extremely thoughtful and thought provoking. In October 2010, he wrote in the *Irish Times* about the failure of government, public service, and property development and asked himself why there had "been such a simultaneous collective collapse in public responsibility in all these areas." His answer: "A striking absence of any sense of civic responsibility throughout our society. The civic morality that underlies the social cohesion of so many democratic societies seems to me to have been absent in Ireland in recent decades."

In a speech given a month earlier, Ireland's president Mary McAleese called for a management system that both recognized and rewarded "good and exceptional performance and, at the same time, tackles under-performance where it arises."

FitzGerald echoed what Jim Sheridan had once told me about the cultural memory of lying being acceptable: "As for the Catholic majority, a society under alien rule cannot be expected to develop a sense of civic responsibility. And a popular church, identifying with its flock, first in opposition to the dominance of a ruling minority of another faith, and then to aspects of an alien government, could not be expected to instill much respect for public authority." He also said that an education system left to the church "was left with virtually no training in civic morality or civic responsibility" and that the value system inherited from that colonial past "undervalued integrity in public life, to such a degree that it has seen tax evasion by a minister as grounds for repeatedly reelecting him to parliament."

Karen Coleman, presenter of the Newstalk radio station's *The Wide Angle*, wrote a book entitled *Haunting Cries*, about the child abuse that occurred in some religious institutions in Ireland. In an October 2010 piece in the *Irish Times*, she wrote about the Irish culture of deference, nepotism, and cronyism: "A blind support of the church and a craven deference to bankers are two symptoms of the same malaise." The Irish people have regularly looked the other way to what the state did, what the church did, what the bankers did, what the civil servants do. It was impossible to see the extravagant lifestyle led by former taoiseach Charles Haughey and reconcile that with his modest annual salary.

Pointless Reports and Conferences

In July 2008, Taoiseach Brian Cowen announced that he had charged his ambassador to the US, Michael Collins, with carrying out a strategic review of the US-Ireland relationship in the post-peace-process era, to see how to "harness" the Irish diaspora.

The timing was interesting. I don't know if it was coincidental or not, but the call for this review came two months after Senator Kennedy had been diagnosed with a malignant brain tumor, from which he would die in August 2009.

For nearly ten years, I had been sounding the alarm about the shifts underway in the relationship. One impetus to my creating the US-Ireland Alliance was something Senator Kennedy said to me around 1997: "What are they going to do when I'm not around anymore?"

Maybe Senator Kennedy's diagnosis was a wake-up call for the Irish government that I had failed to arouse. They knew that a significant part of their getting things done in Washington, DC, was largely due to a small number of people.

An example of this involved President Bill Clinton's first budget proposal, which included a provision that concerned Ireland. In May 1993, Ireland's ambassador to the US, Dermot Gallagher, rang me to ask for Senator Kennedy's help in arranging a meeting for him with Senator Daniel Patrick Moynihan, then chairman of the Senate Finance Committee. Gallagher felt Moynihan was avoiding him regarding the tax deferral issue. Ireland depended heavily (then as now) on US investment, and the Irish were concerned, to simplify a complicated issue, that the Clinton proposal would pull the rug out from under Ireland.

Kennedy asked Moynihan to give Gallagher the courtesy of a meeting but didn't overly involve himself in the issue, as there was concern about helping foreign countries at the expense of the US. Moynihan met Gallagher, and the upshot was that the Irish were satisfied with the outcome. Had it gone a different way, the Celtic Tiger may have been stopped in its tracks. Matters that required assistance in the US—the peace process, immigration, and other issues—were often resolved by senior American politicians with an interest in Ireland.

By the time the Irish government realized it needed to focus on the needs of the relationship, a lot of time had been squandered. While much could have been done during the Celtic Tiger years, the actual release of the ambassador's report on the relationship came in 2009, when the economies of both Ireland and the US had taken disastrous turns.

When the report was commissioned, I reached out to Ambassador Collins, asking if my colleague Mary Lou Hartman and I might meet with him to make some suggestions. I had known Collins during his previous tour in Washington, but this time, I found him fairly disengaged. When Mary Lou and I went to his office, we were greeted with a blasé, "I can write that report in 15 minutes."

In March 2009, the taoiseach released the report entitled "Ireland and America: Challenges and Opportunities in a New Context." After his St. Patrick's Day trip to the US, he stated that the review "includes a number of recommendations that will re-energise and ultimately transform how Ireland does her business in America."

Reports and conferences are endless and fairly useless exercises used to kick issues down the road while giving the appearance of doing something. In fact, the review was too little too late. The nearly forty-page document wasn't visionary. Much of it, along with many things raised a few months later at the first diaspora gathering at Farmleigh—a Guinness family estate in Dublin purchased by the Irish government—was things that were already being done, things that had long been proposed but had never been acted upon, and things that Ireland then didn't have the funds to accomplish.

In 2010, after Farmleigh, Lara Marlowe wrote in the *Irish Times* of Cowen's decision to open a consulate in Atlanta after "Ambassador Michael Collins advocated the establishment of a Consulate General to serve the US southeast in his March 2009 strategic review." But the idea was hardly novel. I mooted it in 2005 in an *Irish Times* piece, and I'd be surprised if it hadn't been raised internally in the Department of Foreign Affairs as well. Again, to justify conferences and reports, old ideas were described as new. I'm delighted there are now consulates in Atlanta and Austin, but neither Farmleigh nor a report was necessary to make that happen.

The report mentioned nearly every organization, ours included, in what read like a laundry list—as if everyone would be flattered to be named and thus say the report was fantastic. Many of its recommendations didn't come close to addressing the various ways in which the world has changed and what that means for the future of the relationship between the United States and Ireland.

Certificates of Irishness

Don Keough, the former CEO of Coca-Cola, was someone who gave a great deal to the US-Ireland relationship prior to his death in 2015. He was a major contributor to Notre Dame, and he was also the first person to contribute to the US-Ireland Alliance in 1998. Nearly ten years later, Don sought my views on an idea he had about extending Irish citizenship to the Scotch Irish in America.

If a person can show that a grandparent is Irish, they can obtain Irish citizenship and an Irish passport. Most of the Scotch Irish came to the US well before the Irish Catholics who left Ireland during the Famine and thus have ancestors too distant to qualify for Irish citizenship. I thought Don's idea of extending this opportunity back to earlier generations wouldn't fly with the Irish government because Ireland would have obligations toward these possible new citizens. Ambassador Collins confirmed that he didn't see Ireland being more generous on this front, and, if anything, the view would more likely be to make it more difficult to get Irish citizenship.

Perhaps Collins had Keough's idea in mind when he suggested in his 2009 report on the relationship that such individuals could be given certificates of Irish ancestry, which, "while having no legal standing as such, would constitute official recognition for many people of their familial and emotional connection with Ireland." Niall O'Dowd's *Irish Central* anticipated that there were "millions of Irish descendants around the world who will apply for these certificates."

The idea of certificates struck me as extremely kitsch. In a blog in 2012, I wrote that I couldn't imagine people would want them, and it was cringeworthy seeing the taoiseach give one to President Obama at the White House St. Patrick's Day party.

Enter Mark Daly, a Fianna Fail Irish senator from County Kerry, a grandstander who is big on photo ops and light on substance. He had a reputation in the US as trying to ingratiate himself with American politicians. Daly was outraged by my blog, or more likely just found it something to grandstand about, and O'Dowd's tabloids were all too happy to run with this. The lead in *Irish Central* on March 24, 2012, was "Leading Irish Pol Calls for Inquiry into US Ireland Alliance Funding after Verbal Attack." James O'Shea reported that Daly was demanding that I appear before the Irish Parliament and that he wanted "an investigation into how Irish taxpayer money is being spent by Vargo and also to question her on attacks she made on Irish leader Enda Kenny and Irish Americans at the

White House last week." Daly suggested I should apologize and that the Irish government should not fund the Mitchell Scholarship program.

I hadn't insulted Kenny but rather whoever suggested he give Obama the certificate. I wonder now if that idea came from Daly. And did anyone believe that Daly, a member of the opposition party, was outraged on behalf of the prime minister from the other party?

Why was Daly such a cheerleader for the certificates? It was down to parish-pump politics. On Daly's own website, it said that he was working with FEXCO, a company in his constituency, which was engaged by the Department of Foreign Affairs to "produce, market, and distribute the Certificate."

Always trying to begin by giving one the benefit of the doubt, I immediately rang Daly to correct any misunderstandings he may have had about the Mitchell Scholarship program. I got his voice mail and left a message. He never returned the call. I certainly didn't mind if he didn't like my blog, but it was another thing to suggest the Alliance had misspent funds. I next emailed Daly to say that no Irish government funds had been spent on the Mitchell Scholarship program in about a decade. Audit reports confirmed that. Therefore, if we hadn't been spending the Irish government's money, it would obviously be impossible for us to be *mis*spending it. Daly never replied.

Ruairi Quinn, Ireland's minister of education, was not going to be drawn into Daly's games. Quinn had received every audit of the Irish government's financial contributions to the Mitchell Scholarship endowment and knew that the only money spent from the endowment was for the annual audit, which was required by the Irish government. If Daly had bothered to read the audit, which he had access to, he'd have known that.

Daly wouldn't let it go. As a member of the Joint Committee on Foreign Affairs and Trade, he got the clerk of the committee to send me an invitation to address the committee. I had the distinct impression that Daly's colleagues also thought him a nuisance but found it easier to humor him than to have him round on them. I was going to be in Ireland in May and offered to meet with the committee chairman.

Before my trip, Daly wrote to Secretary of State Hillary Clinton to complain that I hadn't immediately agreed to come before the Irish Foreign Affairs committee to explain how the Alliance was spending Irish taxpayer money that we actually weren't spending. During a month when Clinton was dealing with things like a Chinese dissident crisis and children being killed in Syria, Mark Daly was asking Clinton to "raise this unsatisfactory situation" (my not replying quickly enough) with the Alliance board and the Friends of Ireland on Capitol Hill.

Daly's letter reminded the secretary that the US government was providing funds for the Mitchell Scholarship program at a time when the administration had already decided to eliminate Mitchell Scholarship funding. Daly's letter seemed intended to strengthen the hand of those who wanted to resist Congressional pressure to restore funding for a prestigious scholarship that was putting Ireland's universities on the map in the US. One document I have received, via a Freedom of Information request with the Department of State, suggests that the Irish embassy in Washington (then under Ambassador Michael Collins) was not exactly supporting the Mitchell program. The source's name is blacked out in a report that career State Department foreign service officer Kathleen Doherty sent to Jake Sullivan, a close Hillary Clinton aide who was then the director of Policy Planning at State. The May 2012 memo says that the source "told us that Senator Daly speaks for himself but also said they have received little detail from the US-Ireland Alliance regarding expenditures of Irish funding." Had received little detail? The Irish government knew that no Irish funds were being spent. This statement was, as the Irish would say, cute. Whoever made this statement to the Department of State was being, at best, economical with the truth. In an *Irish Times* article by Georgina O'Halloran on June 23 (one month after this memo), Taoiseach Kenny said that officials in the Irish embassy in Washington were in touch with the State Department about our funding. As the taoiseach was calling the Mitchell a valuable program, why would embassy officials be briefing State with a misleading, negative spin?

Brian Barrington, a Dublin barrister and member of the Alliance board, joined me in meeting with the chairman of the Foreign Affairs Committee, Pat Breen. We told Breen that we would consider a meeting with the committee, but, given that no Irish government funds had even been spent (something Breen hadn't realized), we were not inclined to respond to silly-season tabloid stories. We settled on an informal meeting, as I was happy to go back and forth with Daly, but I wasn't interested in a format where he could say whatever he liked and I couldn't challenge him in response. A formal hearing in the Oireachtas would have provided Daly with privilege, meaning that he would be free to say whatever he wanted, no matter how false, and we would not have recourse to legal action. Given that Daly had already been warned about making any further false statements about the Alliance, it was our view that he wanted to attack from within the Oireachtas, where he would be shielded from a slander claim.

Daly was next demanding that the foreign minister, Eamon Gilmore, go before the Irish Senate to explain why I hadn't yet appeared. And this was all because I wrote in a blog that said certificates of Irish ancestry were silly. If I were a constituent of Daly's, I'd be asking if my senator hadn't anything better to do with his time.

In August, Newstalk radio presenter Marc Coleman left me a phone message saying he was "following on from the Mark Daly thing . . . questions about the funding you do receive from Government and what sources it is put to. . . . There's a concern whether maybe some of the funding is going towards, you know, politically correct, quote unquote, issues that might be, sort of, I don't know advocating abortion on demand or whatever. There's some question about that. Maybe completely false but I just want to verify with you. . . ." Whoever rang Coleman was just making stuff up. But it does raise the question of why abortion, of all random issues, was pulled out of thin air. And why didn't Coleman demand that his "source" provide even a scintilla of evidence before bothering to ask me such a question. (The choice of abortion feels very much like someone trying to point out that I'm a woman and had worked for Senator Kennedy, a liberal politician. I have come across some men who have an issue with women leaders. In the early days of creating the organization, I met with a man on Wall Street who was a potential funder, given his surname and wealth. He spent our rather brief meeting noticing I wore no wedding ring, telling me how his daughters and daughters-in-law stayed at home and raised children, and asked if I was "one of them there feminists." All of this from my just asking if he'd have any interest in supporting a scholarship that sends students to Ireland.)

Niall O'Dowd's hand in Daly's attacks was not subtle. In *Irish Central* in September 2012, the headline read, "Irish Politician Questions the Actions of the US-Ireland Alliance Regarding the Undocumented Irish." O'Dowd was still obsessed with that opinion piece I had written five years earlier, and Daly was a convenient stalking horse: "Daly also claimed that Vargo was not supportive of the plight of undocumented Irish in the US." And totally overstating my influence,

Daly said, "Her view that no effort should be made to secure a deal for the undocumented Irish unquestionably hinders the current Irish Government's efforts."

Believing I could more than hold my own with Daly, our board members encouraged me to meet with the committee. I was now looking forward to this—perhaps Senator Daly would be able to enlighten me as to what part of zero we were misspending.

Joined by Barrington and another of our board members, Hayes Solicitors' Joe O'Malley, I met with the committee in September 2012. In attendance in addition to the chairman were four TDs: Eric Byrne (Labour), Bernard Durkan (FG), Senator Michael Mullins (FG), and Senator Daly. Except for Daly, the committee members were overwhelmingly supportive and clearly embarrassed by their colleague.

Daly read a short list of things I'd written that he didn't like and wanted me to withdraw them. I refused. He said that some of the things I'd said reflected on officials in the room. The chairman rebuked Daly not to involve anyone in the room. Daly said I was "undiplomatic." He was correct about that at least.

He went on to address Brian and Joe in a way that suggested the board should keep me in check. Daly had no one in the room on his side. Durkan said he didn't know where Senator Daly was coming from, but that most of what I had stated in my opening address pertained to matters with which he strongly agreed, and that he was satisfied that the Alliance showed great results. Byrne joked that my name had been mentioned around the Foreign Affairs Committee more often than the Middle Eastern crisis. He said that he applauded people who stand up for their beliefs and that a large legacy of problems in the history of Ireland arise from not standing up to institutions like the church and persons and entities with strong views.

Barrington said that the point that I'd made in my 2007 opinion piece, that a special deal for Irish people was not politically achievable, proved to be correct, and the only way matters for the Irish would be resolved was through comprehensive immigration reform. He also said that it was a matter of great concern to me, and our board, that opportunities had been missed in the past, and that I was right to comment critically upon these matters.

I told the committee that I welcome criticism but only insofar as it is based upon facts. Daly's criticisms were not. He had never taken me up on my offer to discuss any questions he had. Since this whole matter began, it became more and more clear that Daly had been doing O'Dowd's bidding. In the meeting, he pulled out an email I'd sent to Senator Kennedy six years earlier, an email that only O'Dowd had been given a copy of and which he had been using to misrepresent my views.

Daly said I shouldn't go after those engaged in shamrockery. He said that the special deal was intended to be a mutual deal, which could benefit US citizens seeking to get into Ireland. More nonsense. I've never heard of any Americans illegally in Ireland fighting to stay. Daly again returned to suggesting to Brian and Joe that the board of the Alliance should rein me in.

Defeated, Daly slumped down into his chair like a sulking child. Afterward, several of the members thanked us for turning up. Daly left the room without so much as a handshake.

As I had predicted, no one was interested in those certificates of Irishness. The very next month, the *Irish Times'* Pamela Duncan reported that only a little more than a thousand people purchased one in the past thirteen months.

In August 2015, the *Irish Times* reported that fewer than three thousand were ever purchased and only 150 in that year. The program was discontinued. Niall O'Dowd, whose *Irish Central* predicted millions would buy these, was now telling RTE that he'd predicted that the scheme wouldn't work.

Farmleigh—Talk Shops

I declined to attend the Global Irish Economic Forum (commonly referred to as Farmleigh) in September 2009. I did so privately but agreed completely with the public stance taken by Ryanair CEO, Michael O'Leary, who said, "I wouldn't participate in a three-day photoshoot, listening to the great and the good of the Irish diaspora. . . . I'd happily go along for four hours on a Tuesday in Government Buildings, with no press, no photo-calls, and come up with a list of decisions, and then let's implement them. The problem with this Government is that it's always one forum, one high-level commission and one photo-shoot away from making a decision." O'Leary was spot-on.

Ireland's economy was in the toilet, and this all amounted to a request of the diaspora to extricate Ireland from a situation of its own making. Farmleigh resulted in little more than a rehash of Ambassador Collins's report.

Before deciding to decline the invitation, I asked Joe Hackett, the Irish diplomat in charge of the conference, if this wasn't just another American Ireland Fund event, because it sounded a lot like two previous diaspora conferences sponsored by the American Ireland Fund. I knew of nothing substantive that came from those. The only difference I saw here was that it reached beyond the diaspora in the US, to include others around the world.

Hackett told me that the AIF "has no involvement in the organisation, planning or funding of the Global Irish Economic Forum," and he said that the steering papers were being prepared by the relevant government departments. But someone from the AIF contacted me to tell me they were writing the papers for the conference. The person who called me went on to say the AIF had "a theory that educational exchange should and could play a pivotal role in the diaspora strategy."

Educational exchange was not a "theory," nor was it a new idea. The US-Ireland Alliance had been actively doing this for the previous decade through the Mitchell Scholarship program, as were numerous other programs involving Irish universities and other organizations.

I asked Hackett what the government wanted to see come from such a conference, and he said they had no particular vision. Given the state of the economy, and my doubts about outcomes, I took a pass. I didn't want to be part of an event that was spending taxpayer money on nothing more than a talk shop. Many did spot this for what it was, and there was a lot negatively written about the conference after.

Collins's report did admit to what these exercises were really about: "The current economic downturn represents a timely stimulus to look again at our overseas communities, particularly in the US, and to see how this valuable resource can be elevated to a new and even more dynamic level." Translation: "We're broke. What can you do for us?"

In 2013, Tourism Ireland launched something called "the Gathering," which was meant to get the Irish diaspora to return to Ireland and spend money. Gabriel Byrne called the scheme an attempt to "shake down" Irish Americans "for a few quid." He rightly noted the donor fatigue felt in America.

Much of the report and the conference was indicative of something that is a huge problem in the relationship. For all the talk about an equal relationship, Ireland often doesn't walk the walk. Lip service is sometimes given about the two-way street, and phrases like "mutually beneficial" are trotted out. But the US and the diaspora are mainly treated like a large bank of money, people, markets, etc. from which Ireland wants to extract but to which they rarely want to contribute. I am only now starting to see a slight shift, but only when US funding has dried up.

Universities

Our experience has been that when ideas are suggested, the civil servants hope to steal ideas but not actually work with those who have a track record on delivery. In Collins's report, he wrote, "There are some 10 million Irish Americans under the age of 18 and there are many others who, while not Irish, have an interest in Ireland. There is scope for a coordinated approach among the universities and higher education institutes to publicizing and promoting the higher education sector in Ireland. . . ." And from Farmleigh: "Consideration might be given to the appointment by the Universities of a full-time representative to coordinate their activities in the US."

Seven years before that report was written, one year after the first class of Mitchell Scholars, we had recommended to the Irish universities that they might want to pool together and get a PR firm in the US to promote all the universities on the island. I suggested Amy Seigenthaler. Amy was the head of a Nashville-based PR company, and at the time, she had just returned from Ireland, where she'd been Ambassador Jean Kennedy Smith's aide. Amy seemed the perfect person for such a task, and she even sent a proposal to the universities about how that might work. No one took her up on it.

The country rarely takes advantage of the Mitchell Scholarship program the way it could. The Mitchell is the most prestigious program in the US, and it brings attention to universities in Ireland, but initiatives are nearly always our doing. Exceptions were Marina Donohoe and Michelle Dervan when they handled education for Enterprise Ireland, and recent consuls general in Atlanta (Paul Gleeson) and San Francisco (Philip Grant, and now Robert O'Driscoll). I am noticing a more open and modern approach with the next generation of diplomats, but they are not yet in positions where they have the final say.

It is important that Ireland not lose sight of the significance of a strong third-level educational system. Second to my concern about funding the Mitchell is my concern that Irish universities will dip so far in the global rankings that we'll lose the ability to attract America's best and brightest. There is no dispute that more funding is needed, but politicians resist, under public pressure, reasonable increases in tuition. If governments can't or won't provide the funds necessary, they need to free up the universities to raise money. There is a much greater potential for Irish universities on the world stage, but it requires adequate funding and joined-up thinking.

High School

As a high school student in the US, I never learned about Ireland because it didn't rank up there with the Civil War, French and American Revolutions, WWII, or Vietnam. At the age of seventeen, I went on a trip to France with others in my high school French class. That trip played a large role in my decision to study international affairs and to do my graduate work at McGill University in Montreal. My experiences abroad led to my passion to help provide similar experiences for others, which explains the Mitchell Scholarship program and our nascent high school education program.

Over the years, several US high school teachers have told me that if they had the materials, they'd teach about Ireland. The US-Ireland Alliance has started to develop these materials and provide teachers with them. The going is slow because we have had to raise the funds by online crowd funding.

Since 2007, we've been pitching this idea to the Irish government and some companies. The plan includes the aim of getting high school teachers to take their students to Ireland, as my French teacher took me to France. This would be positive for tourism and could also result in these high school students later deciding to study in Ireland.

Collins's 2009 report suggested that "more could be done to engage Irish and American students at secondary and high school levels." At Farmleigh, the issue of high school education was also raised. It's easy to throw that line out in a report, but we had been providing detailed proposals to the Irish government for years, and no one acted. When I later mentioned that to Collins, he snidely responded, "You should have come to Farmleigh."

Again, the Irish embassy put out a report in the spring of 2014 called "Ireland and America: Challenges and Opportunities in a New Context." It was less of the same. Short on specifics. No big ideas. More marketing-speak: "We are still in search of an over-arching brand for Ireland," and mention of the desire to commission a "perceptions review"—another report that will lead to another conference that will lead to very little.

Prime Minister Varadkar has said he wants to expand Ireland's footprint around the world. While more embassies, consulates, and diplomats may be a good thing, that doesn't constitute a strategy.

"And I shall have some peace there"— the Aftermath of September 11

I previously mentioned our Innisfree Fund and that many people had come together to send to Ireland the families of the police officers and firemen who died on September 11. A recurrent issue in dealing with state bodies is that the deal is never the deal. Aer Lingus ultimately provided a special rate on flights, but not before trying to squeeze us. We originally reached out to several airlines, told them what we were planning to do, and asked for rate quotes. Three airlines submitted proposals, and Aer Lingus's was the lowest, by just a bit. Before the offers were in, Ryanair CEO, Michael O'Leary, generously offered to fly families free from the UK if we ended up going with a carrier that did not offer a direct flight to Ireland. It was only after we declined two other offers and accepted the Aer Lingus offer that Dan Loughrey, in charge of marketing at Aer Lingus, came back to me to say that, oh, by the way, that quote didn't include taxes, so we'd have to add another hundred dollars to the price of each ticket! That amount of money meant that the other two carriers had made better offers than Aer Lingus, and we'd already turned them down. Several people, including Bill Shipsey, a senior barrister who was then on our board, and the taoiseach's staff, were part of the conversation that took place in the taoiseach's office, and all were equally stunned by what Aer Lingus was attempting to do. Loughrey told me I could just go raise more money. I told him I couldn't, and I wouldn't, and I expected that Aer Lingus would abide by the commitment that was made. This dragged on for some time. Finally, I had to bring an end to it. In Dublin, I was walking up Grafton Street to the Westbury Hotel where I was to be interviewed by a journalist with the Irish magazine *Business and Finance*. I rang Loughrey en route and told him we'd had enough—either he confirmed that the deal was the deal, or I would tell the journalist all about it in the interview I was about to do. It took that level of brinkmanship before Loughrey finally agreed to do what he'd promised.

Ultimately, more than one hundred families (five hundred individuals) availed of the offer and visited various parts of the island for one week. The first family to participate arrived in Ireland in July 2002. Sheila and Rosemarie Langone met Garda commissioner Pat Byrne and assistant chief fire officer Hugh O'Neill in Dublin. Mrs. Langone lost two sons, and Rosemarie two brothers, in the World Trade Center on September 11. Peter

Langone was a member of the New York City Fire Department, and his brother, Thomas, was a member of the New York City Police Department. The Langones received a warm welcome in Dublin, Waterford, Cork, and Kenmare.

Everyone was a winner in the initiative. Everyone who gave did so for the purest of reasons, and the unintended benefit was that all these Americans were spending money in Ireland at a time when tourism from the US was reduced. We found that, in addition to what we offered families, many of them brought other family members. And the program resulted in nearly $240,000 worth of ticket sales for Aer Lingus.

If you have integrity, nothing else matters. If you don't have integrity, nothing else matters.

—Senator Alan Simpson

Chapter 5

IN THE ROUGH

Fintan Drury, the Ryder Cup, and the Long Grass

"They'll be waiting for you in the long grass" is a phrase the Irish like to use to refer to someone who has it out for you but who will lie in wait to exact their revenge when you're not expecting it. I was told this on more than one occasion, including in relation to Fintan Drury.

Drury is a public relations man in Dublin who founded Drury Communications and Platinum One, a sports event management company. He was also a nonexecutive board member of Anglo Irish Bank just prior to its collapse and was closely associated with the then CEO of Anglo, Sean Fitzpatrick. Drury had a reputation of loving to brag about his political connections with Fianna Fail, particularly Brian Cowen, who, in 2006, was Ireland's finance minister and deputy prime minister.

For many years beginning in 1999, the US-Ireland Alliance annually held a golf tournament at the K Club in Straffan, County Kildare, just outside of Dublin. The purpose of the event was to introduce senior American business leaders to their counterparts in Ireland in hopes that business relationships would be formed.

At one tournament dinner, we sat Paul Nolan, then director of the Irish Pub Company, next to Phil Lengyel, then VP of Development at Walt Disney World in Florida. A conversation began that evening that led to the establishment of the Raglan Road Irish Pub and Restaurant at Disney World. Nolan later told me that the multimillion-dollar development helped the US economy by employing 275 people and was one of the top twenty highest-grossing restaurants in the US. The project also benefited Ireland because millions of euros were spent there on the pub's development and on the purchase of Irish produce. The restaurant employs Irish graduates in management positions. It also employs Irish musicians and dancers. Additionally, they take their top twenty employees to Ireland for a week each year to learn about Irish culture. It is also the top seller of Guinness in the US.

In the summer of 2003, when we learned that the 2006 Ryder Cup would be held on the Arnold Palmer–designed course at the K Club, we decided to hold our own golf tournament there just after. We would invite the Americans over early to attend the competition, which was being held for the first time in Ireland.

As hospitality suites at the tournament cost €150,000, this was not something we undertook lightly. That is a lot of money for a small nonprofit organization. After much research and discussion, we partnered with an Irish company to share the suite and halve our costs; we concluded this was a worthwhile investment in showing off Ireland on this unique sporting occasion. Sponsors of our tournament would cover the costs, and it was a win-win in that the Americans would get to attend the premiere golfing event and Ireland would benefit from the tourism spend that would come with our event. For the first time ever, Europe would win its third consecutive Ryder Cup in a tournament laden with emotion, given that Irish golfer Darren Clarke's wife, Heather, had died of cancer just two months earlier.

Ruth Shipsey, a Dublin solicitor, avid golf fan, and a member of our board, began a conversation in the summer of 2003 with Fintan Drury, John Burke, and Mark Lee about purchasing a suite at the Ryder Cup, as Drury's company, Platinum One, was selling the suites. We agreed to the purchase only after the suite's exact location on the course was confirmed. Several suites are contained within a large tent (basically, several suites within a suite). A suite is a room where meals are catered and one can escape inclement weather and watch the action on television. That would come in handy, as the tournament got off to a blustery, rain-soaked start. Like seats at any event, some are better than others. Just as one wouldn't pay the price of an orchestra seat to sit in the balcony of a theater, or pay for box seats to sit in the nosebleed section of a sports stadium, the same goes for suites on fairways at golf tournaments. We purchased our suite in what was part of the larger Liffey Suite on the seventeenth fairway, the next-to-the-last hole on the golf course. The suites on the eighteenth fairway had already been reserved. The seventeenth was the next best location, and it included a view of the action on the seventeenth green. In January 2005, Platinum One invoiced us for this specific suite, confirming in writing our location on the course.

But just days before the tournament began, Platinum One attempted to deliver to Ruth Shipsey tickets to an entirely different suite on a different fairway. Ruth explained that those were not the tickets we purchased, and she wisely refused to accept them. We made multiple attempts to get Platinum

One to provide what was contracted. We were clearly being bumped, but there was never an explanation as to who had been given our suite. Platinum One told us that Ryder Cup Europe made the decision to move us and there was nothing they could do. When I spoke with David Watt, a Ryder Cup Europe official in Wentworth, Surrey, England, he claimed that Drury's company was promising something it had no business promising. I noted that Platinum One was the agent of the Ryder Cup European Tour and that the Tour could not simply dissociate itself from the actions of its agents. Emails going back three years clearly indicated that Wentworth had been consulted and had approved our suite location.

Watt made a feeble attempt to convince me that the suite we were now offered was just as good. He also said we could cancel, but that was quite impossible, as our guests were flying to Ireland for the tournament within days.

Watt quickly went into damage-control mode and was keen to know what we planned to do. I told him that we would like to receive the tickets we purchased. Failing that, we would have no choice but to take legal action. He asked what I would say to the press. The facts, I told him. An agreement had been made, and that agreement was now being broken. Watt wanted to know how I would "prove" that. The emails would clearly tell the story, as would our invoice, which specified our location on the course. Grasping at this point, he asked if he had been copied on the emails. As we had always and only dealt directly with Platinum One, it was absurd to suggest that we would have copied emails to someone we didn't even know.

Watt then asked if we possessed our tickets. I informed him that Platinum One attempted to deliver the tickets, but that Ruth did not accept them. Watt went silent. I had the feeling that he assumed we had those tickets in our possession and that he was hoping to say that possession indicated acceptance.

We were left with no choice but to quickly seek an injunction in the High Court, as our real objective was simply to get the tickets we bought. While we didn't win the immediate injunction, Judge Frank Clarke, who would later become the chief justice of Ireland's Supreme Court, gave every indication that this was not for the lack of a good case. He said that if he ordered us to be positioned where contracted, some other group would have to be moved to facilitate us, and at that stage, he couldn't know who was in "our" suite; if he bumped another group, then they too might have a cause of action and apply to the court seeking injunction. The judge indicated sympathy with our position during the course of his ruling, when he refused, "with considerable regret," to grant the injunction. We understood his predicament, so we were left with no option but to use a different suite for the Ryder Cup and seek damages later.

Inexplicably, instead of just settling the case and putting it behind him, Drury allowed the matter to drag on for nearly a year. At no time did he ever contact me, nor was there an apology or an explanation as to why Platinum One broke the contract. At one stage, Niall O'Dowd rang me (this was before he fell out with me in 2007) because Drury had been onto him, seeking to use O'Dowd as some sort of interlocutor. I told O'Dowd that if Drury wanted to speak with me, he could ring me himself, but there really wasn't anything to discuss at that stage. The case was before the court, it was an open-and-shut case, and my advice was that Drury settle it and save himself a lot of legal fees.

Finally, in September 2007, Drury's Platinum One paid damages in addition to fees to Hayes Solicitors, who acted for us. Drury settled only when the next step in the process would have required him to divulge the names of the others who were in the tent on the seventeenth. A simple matter of checking dates on invoices and contracts would make clear for whom we had been bumped.

Drury was not happy. At one dinner party in Dublin, he was heard to say, in reference to funding the Irish government had committed to our Mitchell Scholarship program, that he was a good friend of Brian Cowen and that he would do everything he could to make sure we didn't get that money. He also bragged that someone had been planning to give $1 million for the scholarship endowment but that he had stopped that from happening. Drury's company broke a contract, and instead of being embarrassed and sorry, he spoke of vengeance against a nonprofit organization that he screwed.

In 2006, Bertie Ahern and Brian Cowen had committed that the Irish government would match any funds, up to €20 million, raised by the US-Ireland Alliance toward the establishment of a permanent endowment for the Mitchell Scholarship program. On the basis of that commitment, we had quickly raised nearly $2 million.

For years, the Irish government had not provided the match, claiming that new legislation was required. It took years to draft a simple piece of legislation. Officials in Ireland's Department of Education asked me to write the first draft of that legislation in 2007, and it then took them nine months just to reply. At one point, the minister of education, Batt O'Keeffe, suggested that this had taken so long because of "protracted" negotiations with the Alliance. The Alliance had responded promptly at every stage of the process—the only thing that had been protracted was his department's response time. And the delay could not be attributed to the economic downturn because funds were provided in budgets; they were just never paid until the summer of 2010.

For the Irish embassy in Washington, DC, St. Patrick's Day is a big occasion, including a party at the ambassador's residence that the taoiseach attends every year. At the 2008 party,

I made both Gerry Hickey and Ambassador Collins aware of what I was told Drury had been saying around Dublin. I had always found Hickey, a longtime adviser to Taoiseach Bertie Ahern, to be direct and decent. Gerry concurred that Drury was in fact a friend of Cowen's, but he felt that there was a public commitment to the Mitchell Scholarship program and that it would be honored without question. Collins's advice was that I should probably make Joe Lennon, Ahern's press spokesman, aware of this as well. I made clear that I assumed there was nothing Drury could do, but I thought they should be made aware, as it wasn't good for Cowen to have someone running around suggesting the deputy prime minister would use his office to settle scores for friends.

Two months later, Cowen became taoiseach when Bertie Ahern resigned. That same month, I was in Ireland for the conclusion of the academic year for the Mitchell Scholars on the island. As Cowen was new to his job and had many things on his plate, I did not seek to meet with him, but instead met Joe Lennon, who was then working for Cowen. Before seeing Joe, I met with Martin Mansergh, a member of the Irish Parliament who had been tapped by Cowen to serve as minister of state in the Department of Finance. I had known Martin for years, having worked with him on the Northern Ireland peace process. When I told him of Drury's reported threats, he agreed that I should make Joe Lennon aware. When I told Martin of Drury's comment to third parties, "Does she know who I am?" Martin joked that I was formidable myself: "Does he know who *you* are?" When I met Joe for lunch near Leinster House, he confirmed that Drury and Cowen were close, but he found Drury's suggestions outrageous and told me he would let Cowen know what Drury had been saying.

In addition to bragging about his efforts to prevent the Irish government from fulfilling its legal obligation to the Mitchell endowment, Drury also bragged that he stopped a $1 million donation to the Scholarship. At the time, the only such discussion being held was with CRH. The construction materials company was the largest Irish company with a presence in nearly every state in the US, and we had hoped that it would lead the way with the first such corporate contribution.

Over the years, CRH had supported the Mitchell Scholarship program with $20,000 annually. My main contact at the company was Jack Golden, who was the Group HR director and the lead role in philanthropy for the company. I kept him abreast of developments with the Mitchell Scholarship program, and he was always supportive.

In 2007, CRH's initial commitment of $20,000 a year for five years was coming to an end. I was in touch with Jack about two things: Could we, at a minimum, continue to receive the annual funding, and might we explore the possibility of a $1 million endowment contribution? Over a lunch at the Unicorn, a popular Italian restaurant in Dublin, Jack said CRH was willing to consider the endowment possibility, and he promised that the company would, at a minimum, continue the annual support.

Throughout the rest of the year, there was back-and-forth on the endowment issue. Despite Jack's assurance of the continuation of the annual contribution, the payment never came. As I believed CRH was contemplating a much larger donation, I didn't push for the payment in July (the time they normally paid), but 2007 ended with no check for $20,000 and no explanation.

In May 2008, I had been scheduled to meet with Liam O'Mahony, the CEO of CRH. At the last minute, Jack took the meeting with me instead. He told me he'd know by July about the endowment. I asked him if Fintan Drury had anything to do with this. Golden didn't deny that could be the case; he simply said he didn't *know* that to be the case, and he didn't seem surprised by my question.

And that was the last we heard from CRH. We were never informed that the Mitchell would not receive further annual contributions. They simply ended. And there was no further conversation about the endowment.

(Six years later, in 2014, CRH returned to providing the Mitchell with support [for two years] after Senator Mitchell and I met with Jack in Dublin. By this point, CRH had a new CEO, and Drury's connections with Fianna Fail, which had fallen from favor after the 2008 economic crash, seemed less valuable.)

The Irish are too inclined to defeatism. Sean Lemass complained in 1960 that the main weakness of the Irish character was an "undue disposition to be sorry for ourselves." . . . Because we believe the béal bocht blarney about being deprived and handicapped, we expect others to swallow it as well. We do contribute very generously to causes in the Third World but we also expect our EU neighbors to transfer significant amounts of income to us. . . . We give small, receive big and, on both counts, clap ourselves on the back. . . . Structural Funds . . . Marshall Aid . . . Common Agricultural Policy . . . To date none of these transfers has lessened our appetite for still more aid. . . . Irish defeatism is not justified. We have the resources to address our difficulties.

—Cathal Guiomard, *The Irish Disease*
and How to Cure It

Chapter 6

THE BEGGING BOWL

Ireland and Northern Ireland are wealthy. Yet political leaders from both places have come to the US in search of financial assistance and favors that they should have dropped long ago. There is more to be gained by changing this approach.

The International Fund for Ireland

In November 1985, the Irish and British prime ministers, Garret FitzGerald and Margaret Thatcher, signed the Anglo-Irish Agreement, which was meant to help bring an end to the Troubles in Northern Ireland. As part of an effort to support the Agreement, the two governments created the International Fund for Ireland (IFI) to promote economic and social advancement and reconciliation between the Unionist and Nationalist communities in Northern Ireland and in the border counties. The US Congress agreed to fund the IFI for a period of five years, but it continued to be funded well beyond those five years, and the American taxpayer has contributed more than $530 million, according to the Congressional Research Service's Kristin Archick.

While the IFI was not without value in the early years, it became a tap of easy money from foreign governments, primarily the US, which the British and Irish governments did not want to turn off.

At least as far back as 1995, IFI chairman Willie McCarter told Senator Kennedy that they were going to stop seeking US funds within the next year or two. The former head of Fruit of the Loom in Ireland said he recognized that the IFI had done its job, it didn't need US taxpayers' money anymore, and they just needed to finish projects in the pipeline. The problem was that IFI chairmen said, "Just one more year," year after year.

Senator Kennedy stopped urging his colleagues to support funding for the IFI not long after the Northern Ireland peace agreement was achieved in 1998. He had simply come to the conclusion that the IFI had served its purpose. Also, Ireland had become a wealthy country and didn't need what amounted to development aid from the US.

The IFI had run out of relevant projects and began spending funds on local pet projects that were a far stretch from what was intended and were things the British, Irish, and Northern Ireland governments wouldn't fund themselves. In 2010, SDLP minister Margaret Ritchie conceded she had no idea why the US was giving money to the IFI. When we met in Washington, she had just been on the train from New York City that passes through Philadelphia and Baltimore on the way to Washington, DC, and she noted that the state of our urban housing was much worse than that in Northern Ireland. I was reminded of her comment when the *New York Times* carried a piece in 2012 called "Empire of the In-Between" about the Amtrak industrial corridor. Adam Davidson wrote, "As anyone who rides Amtrak between New York and Washington knows, the trip can be a

dissonant experience. Inside the train, it's all tidy and digital
... while outside the windows an entirely different world glides
by. Traveling south is like moving through a curated exhibit of
urban and industrial decay."

There is a long list of waste on dubious IFI projects, such
as a traveling cinema and a hiking trail. Money was spent on
the Navan Centre, an archaeological site in County Meath
that opened in 1993 but closed in 2001 due to lack of visitors.
A Northern Ireland auditor subsequently concluded that the
forecasts of 160,000 annual visitors for the multimillion-dollar
center had been "unrealistic." The average number was 33,000.

Carl O'Brien wrote in the *Irish Times* in June 2004 that
the IFI contributed "€500,000 towards a coffee shop, retail
facilities to complement the Highlanes Gallery project in
Drogheda." I've been there. It's a lovely art gallery and coffee
shop in Ireland, but I can't for the life of me see how it helped
build ties between communities related to the Troubles.

In June 2004, Patsy McArdle wrote in the *Irish Independent*
that the IFI Board "approved an allocation of €633,000 for an
international school for peace studies in Messines, Belgium."
Again, not remotely what the International Fund for Ireland
money was meant to be spent on.

It was particularly bizarre that US taxpayers were paying
for these things at the height of the economic boom in Ireland
and when Northern Ireland had so much money to burn that,
as Dan Keenan reported in July 2004 in the *Irish Times*, "some
£220 million of unspent government money would be available
in the next financial year."

Instead of wrapping things up, the IFI did what it always
does: announced a pivot. In February 2005, Alison Healy
reported in the *Irish Times* that "a fund that was originally set
up to counter high levels of unemployment and disadvantage
in Northern Ireland and the Border counties is now shifting its focus to reconciliation work, because of the economic

boom." Outgoing IFI chairman Willie McCarter, who had told Senator Kennedy years earlier that the IFI would stop asking for money, decided more ways could be found to spend easy money from American members of Congress who weren't carefully scrutinizing.

In January 2006, Colm Keena reported in the *Irish Times* that McCarter's successor, Denis Rooney, announced a new five-year plan, saying the IFI's "resources might now be more usefully applied to help people live together amicably." The IFI was going nowhere soon. Rooney said, "We want to ensure that the fund will not jog gently to a passive sunset but will continue to take risks on behalf of the communities and deliver the full quarter century of effective intervention." But at least an end date was finally stated: "Over the remaining four years of the fund's life, the board wishes to signal an intention of assisting communities who wish to explore these themes with us." Six years after that statement, yet another five-year plan was announced.

Some were noticing the waste. In April 2006, Sean O'Driscoll wrote in the *Irish Times* that a report launched by Republican senator John McCain referred to the US government's contribution to the IFI as "this year's biggest waste of taxpayers' money on foreign projects." The annual report by the Citizens Against Government Waste (CAGW), known as the "Congressional Pig Book," cites wasteful US government spending, referred to as pork. The report noted, "The US government was 'flushing away' money by funding the World Toilet Summit in Belfast through the IFI."

On October 14, 2009, Maeve Connolly wrote in the Belfast *Irish News* that the IFI "has been criticised after accusations it offered £300,000 to a community organisation which works with loyalist paramilitary groups without checking claims made in its application form." Several people and organizations that allegedly endorsed the project knew nothing of it.

But perhaps the worst example of IFI waste is the so-called Clinton Centre. The person who conceived of this white elephant was Stella O'Leary.

In May 2001, it was announced that the grandiose-sounding William Jefferson Clinton International Peace Centre was to be built on the site of the IRA bombing in Enniskillen, County Fermanagh. The BBC reported that "the new centre will focus on peace-building in Ireland and overseas and will cement a long-term relationship between Mr Clinton and the province." But there was nothing to suggest that O'Leary's vanity project was grounded in any practical reality.

By 2005, the building (reports suggest it cost around $3 million) was turned into a youth hostel. I visited myself to confirm and found the hostel, a café, and a community art gallery on the premises. While O'Leary previously loved to take credit for the project, the self-congratulation and her detailed lengthy vision for the Centre that was on her Irish American Democrats website vanished.

One had to dig for obscure references to the building in IFI annual reports. In the 2003 report, there was a section called the "community bridges" program in an appendix with a line item of £300,000 for the Fermanagh District Council Area. By process of elimination, it appears those were funds for the Clinton Centre. At the exchange rate at the time, that was nearly half a million dollars. It seemed like someone, perhaps foreseeing the unlikely success of the project, wanted to bury it in the reports from the start.

As of this writing, even the hostel seems to be gone. While the expenditure was a total waste of money from day one, Secretary of State Hillary Clinton did reward Ms. O'Leary in 2011 with the title of "Alternate Observer" to the International Fund for Ireland, a position meant to assure that the US taxpayers' contributions to the IFI were well spent. You can't make this stuff up.

Even Clinton aides were, amongst themselves, raising questions.

On December 19, 2011, Amitabh Desai, director of foreign policy for the Clinton Foundation, and formerly a legislative aide to then senator Hillary Clinton, emailed his colleagues about the Clinton Centre. As the email was copied to John Podesta, it was released by Wikileaks in the lead-up to the 2016 presidential campaign. Desai asks the others if they are "comfortable" with O'Leary using Bill Clinton's name to raise funds "for a program at the Clinton Centre in Enniskillen that would connect youth in Northern Ireland and Kosovo." Desai raises "reputational" concerns and seems to recognize that the Centre had largely been a bust by saying that this particular program "actually IS worthwhile." Desai went on: "Unless we want to pull WJC's name from the Centre (which now operates alongside a youth hostel), then it probably would be good to build up the substantive good works of the center (such as this program). Alternatively, if we want to consider pulling WJC's name from the Centre entirely, one of us or someone we trust should go do a site visit. It's nearly impossible (and probably ill advised) to make that decision without seeing the Centre first with our own eyes."

The conflict of interest is obvious. In January 2011, O'Leary was named to observe the IFI, a job that she got thanks to Secretary Clinton. Yet, the request Desai refers to is a December 2011 letter O'Leary wrote to him about her raising funds for the Centre: "I have volunteered to organize a support group in the US to help raise funds for them. This Friends of the Clinton Centre would solicit funds from existing Northern Ireland funding agencies, The International Fund for Ireland, the American Ireland Fund, the British Council (they have already committed) and the Dublin Dept. of Foreign Affairs which has expressed an interest in helping. We will also solicit money from private corporations and interested individuals."

So, while O'Leary was an Observer to the IFI, under the auspices of the State Department, she was seeking funds from the IFI for her own failed pet project.

In the 2008 and 2009 annual reports of the IFI, Chairman Denis Rooney stated explicitly that, as of 2010, the IFI would not be seeking any further international contributions. The Irish government's own report on the future of US-Ireland relations, released by Taoiseach Brian Cowen in 2009, also noted that this initiative was coming to an end. The report, penned by Irish ambassador Michael Collins, suggested that "it would certainly be worthwhile exploring . . . new forms of cooperation. . . ."

The House of Representatives' appropriators' fiscal year 2010 Foreign Operations conference report, passed by the House in December 2009, said, "The conferees expect that the assistance provided in this Act will be the final United States contribution to the IFI."

When the IFI chairman and the Irish government publicly acknowledged that the funding was coming to an end, we at the US-Ireland Alliance decided to ask Congress to match the Irish government's commitment to the Mitchell Scholarship endowment. We approached Capitol Hill with a request for $5 million annually, for four years. Such a contribution would be matched by the Irish government (which had unanimously passed legislation to do so) and would provide for the program in perpetuity.

As the IFI had regularly been receiving between $15 and $20 million a year, we noted that this would still "save" the US Treasury between $40 and $60 million over the period. For those who wished to see the United States contribute to a future relationship with the island of Ireland, this approach provided a way to do so, while at the same time supporting educational opportunities for Americans. And given the Irish government's report reference to seeking new ways to cooperate, we assumed the Irish ambassador to the US would be supportive of the initiative.

On January 25, 2010, I invited Ambassador Collins to lunch at an Italian restaurant not far from the Irish embassy in Washington. I explained our idea. At no time did Collins suggest that the Department of Foreign Affairs might be opposed to this. (I would learn much later that just days before our lunch, Collins met with a staffer of Congressman Jason Chaffetz (R-UT) and also told him that Ireland would not be seeking any more IFI funds.) The only thing Collins asked me at lunch was, "Did you ask the Northerners?" referring to the Northern Ireland political leaders. I told him I saw no reason to, given the IFI chairman's statement, which I showed him. Soon after our meeting (definitely before February 10), I started hearing from staffers on Capitol Hill that Orla O'Hanrahan, Collins's deputy at the Irish embassy, had been contacting them to undermine our effort, saying that the Irish government still wanted the funding, regardless of what the chairman of the IFI wrote in his reports. I had been very upfront with Collins and told him what we were doing. He did not give me the same courtesy. Weeks after I spoke with him, and still not having heard a word directly from him of any opposition, I emailed him to ask if the taoiseach, Brian Cowen, would weigh in on behalf of our effort during his St. Patrick's Day visit to Washington. Collins simply never responded. It wasn't until June, five months after our lunch, that Collins replied that the Northern Ireland Executive and the Irish government "have since decided to request a continuation of IFI funding." So much for the independence of the International Fund for Ireland.

In October, I traveled to Ireland for the arrival of a class of Mitchell Scholars. Their year kicked off with a reception at University College Cork, and the minister for foreign affairs, Micheál Martin, gave remarks. I have huge admiration for Martin's achievement, as health minister, of banning smoking in pubs. That was not a popular decision at the time, and it prompted me to nominate him for the John F. Kennedy Library's Profile in Courage Award. Martin has always been supportive of the Mitchell Scholarship program and the Alliance. At the Cork reception, he raised the IFI funding issue with me. He had clearly heard from Collins on this. It was too much to go into at a reception, but I promised I would explain, which I did within days.

The climate in Congress, exemplified by the Tea Party movement, was about spending as little as possible. The IFI was an easy thing to attack in terms of waste and as a means to embarrass those who had supported it. And the US government was also to blame for not turning off this tap ages ago. Some Republicans introduced a bill specifically "to prohibit contributions to the International Fund for Ireland." This was just not a winning issue for Ireland.

During this time, there was a Committee on Foreign Affairs hearing in the House of Representatives on Northern Ireland and Bosnia. One witness was a woman from Northern Ireland's Committee on the Administration of Justice, Aideen Gilmore. In eight pages of remarks, never once did she mention the IFI as a critical component of the peace process. One witness referred to the IFI once, and in the past tense. If continuance of the IFI was so important and crucial to the peace process, why didn't these witnesses mention it and encourage continued funding?

One Republican congressman rolled his eyes about the $500 million already spent on the IFI and asked if the future shouldn't now be in Northern Ireland's hands. He gave Gilmore a chance to ask for IFI funding and to say how important Congress's contribution to the program was, but she simply didn't bite. She talked about political support from the US but not financial.

Congressman Joe Crowley (D-NY), one of the staunchest advocates for continued IFI funding, focused his remarks on the Bill of Rights and the British constitution. He did say he supported the IFI and also gave Gilmore a chance to thank Congress for IFI money and ask for its continuance, but she didn't. When I later asked Crowley's staffer why the congressman continued to support funding, he couldn't come up with an answer.

Fast forward to September 2015, when the latest tranche of Hillary Clinton's emails was released. The presumptive Democratic nominee for the 2016 race for the presidency was mired in controversy over the fact that, as secretary of state, she used a private server for her emails, thus keeping them out of the hands of the Department of State and the press, who might try to obtain them with Freedom of Information Act requests. Bit by bit, emails were being released to the public.

One of those emails, dated March 18, 2010, was from Kris Balderston to Secretary Clinton. Balderston was in the Department of State as her "Special Representative for Global Partnerships." In 2008, after I helped the Obama campaign, Balderston became noticeably cool and then icy. (Balderston was the man who told me about the special place in hell reserved for those not supporting Hillary.) Given a variety of things, including Melanne Verveer's comments, I had no doubt that I was on the so-called enemies list, so Kris's 2010 email to Secretary Clinton wasn't really a surprise to me. He wrote:

> Spoke to Joe and he is on board and all set re IFI. One concern is that Trini Vargo (frmr EMK staffer) is trying to redirect money from IFI to her Irish Am Alliance for Mitchell scholarships. She will not succeed.

("Joe" referred to Congressman Joe Crowley, a big Hillary Clinton supporter and defender of the IFI; "frmr EMK staffer" reminded Clinton that I had worked for Ted Kennedy, also out of favor with the Clintons for backing Obama.)

This email was sent not long after my lunch with Collins and months before I was told that the Irish government was not going to support our request. Balderston was falsely suggesting I was trying to redirect funds from the International Fund for Ireland. But you can't redirect zero. Remember, the IFI had said it wasn't asking for any more funding, Taoiseach Brian Cowen's 2009 report recognized the end of the IFI was near, and House appropriators said they were finished funding the IFI. President Obama had also not requested funding in the budget proposal he'd just sent to the Hill. If it was so important to Secretary Clinton, why didn't she just put funding for the IFI in the budget?

Why was Balderston even talking to Congressman Crowley about IFI funding? Why were Crowley and a few others determined to fight for funding for something the recipients said they didn't want? And why was Balderston so intent that I would not succeed?

A common refrain from anyone seeking money for Northern Ireland was always that this would keep things from going back to the bad old days. But there was nothing to suggest IFI funds did anything to prevent any violence by remaining thugs hell-bent on criminality. Sectarian violence had decreased markedly. If you remove from the equation intra-community killings, from 2007 through 2011, three people were killed in sectarian-related murders in Northern Ireland. While these deaths were totally unacceptable, the International Fund for Ireland money wouldn't have made any difference. Compare that with an average of about 450 killed each year, during those same years, in Chicago. Even if you adjust for the size of the populations of Chicago and Northern

Ireland, it would still have been 279 murders in Chicago to 3 in Northern Ireland.

Given that many Hill staffers had told me the IFI funding was ending, I had hoped the Irish government would declare victory, thank the US government, and advocate for the contribution to the Mitchell Scholarship program. This kind of approach would have been in line with the constant statements of the Irish government about how Ireland had changed. On April 1, 2009, Taoiseach Cowen told the Irish Parliament, "It is an important point that needs to be made rather than characterising the relationship as Ireland being less than an equal, where it must go cap in hand to the United States." Maybe that was an April Fool's joke. They were still asking for the IFI funding, just under the radar.

Every November, we hold the selection process for the Mitchell Scholarships in Washington on the weekend before Thanksgiving. The Irish ambassador, as part of our funding agreement with the Irish government, is meant to serve on our selection committee, and the Irish embassy is traditionally the site of the reception for finalists, alums, and friends of the program. But in October 2010, a colleague of mine who had been working with the embassy on the event informed me that she was finding Ambassador Collins's assistant oddly cagey about nailing down the details. We were about to send out save-the-date invitations for the reception, but the assistant was saying vague things like, "He may be traveling." It was at this point that I wondered if Minister Martin had shared my recent briefing with Collins. I didn't care if he had, but if that was the case, it would explain the runaround we were now getting.

I emailed Collins and said there seemed to be "a bit of confusion" and that his assistant seemed to be unclear about the selection weekend. I was suspicious but gave him the benefit of the doubt, recognizing there had been some recent personnel changes in the embassy.

I quickly received his terse reply: "No confusion. My availability is uncertain. Will revert next week. . . ." I replied to clarify, "But there is no confusion about the embassy as the site of reception? It's just you in terms of uncertainty?" Then, confirmation of what I suspected when Collins shot back: "I have just been reading your highly derogatory and offensive comments about this Embassy in your letter to Minister Martin. As I say, I'll revert next week." It was Collins who had his minister raise the issue with me, but he didn't like my frank reporting to Martin, which included a reference to Collins's sneaky behavior of sending his staff to the Hill to brief against our effort and not telling me directly that he had a problem with our plans.

I replied to Collins that we couldn't allow the Mitchell Scholarship program to be held hostage to his petty annoyance with me. I had understood that the use of the embassy for the reception was a statement of support on behalf of the government for the Mitchell Scholarship program, not the personal gift of the ambassador. I told him I was clearly mistaken about that and, because we were about to send out invites next week, I would arrange for the reception to be held elsewhere.

I immediately reached out to the British embassy because we also send Mitchell Scholars to Northern Ireland universities. While the British ambassador would be out of town on our date, the deputy chief of mission, Dominick Chilcott (who would later become the UK ambassador to Ireland) graciously offered to host the reception at his residence in northwest Washington.

My exchanges with Collins occurred just before the weekend, and by Monday he realized either that he was out of line altogether or, more likely, that he'd just made the mistake of putting his pique in an email. He came back to me, more diplomatically this time, saying that while he strongly disagreed with "the tone and references to this Embassy" in my memo, "for the record, we continue to value and support the work of the Mitchell Scholars Programme and the Embassy continues to be available to you for the Reception. At this stage, however, I cannot commit regarding my own availability." But the die was cast, and we had the reception at Chilcott's home, and Collins avoided serving on the selection committee for the Mitchell Scholarship program that year.

In more of the emails later released, Stella O'Leary wrote to Cheryl Mills, Secretary Clinton's chief of staff, saying, "Unfortunately, the relentless attacks on the Fund by Ms. Vargo are having an effect on the Hill and we are working hard to counter her irrational obsession with terminating the Fund." She went on to tell Mills, "It would be very helpful if the Secretary would mention her support to Sens. Kerry, Leahy, Durbin, etc. . . ." (O'Leary's definition of "irrational" seemed to be anyone who disagreed with her.)

On April 1, O'Leary emailed Mills again "to crave a favor." O'Leary wrote that the Republicans zeroed out the funding for the IFI for 2011 "at the prompting of Glenn Beck, Rep. Chaffetz of Utah and Trina Vargo. I spent this week cajoling our Republican friends on the Hill, i.e. Reps. Peter King, Chris Smith and Tim Murphy, to restore all or part of the funding," and she goes on to request that Clinton call King to remind him that this matters to her. Suddenly I was part of a right-wing conspiracy.

Mills replied, "Will see what we can do—we are in the budget fight of our lives . . . so not sure how 'use of political capital' wise this fits but will try." Stella wrote back that given King's Irish constituency, he wouldn't want to be "associated with denying the Irish the funding." But there was no "constituency" for IFI funding, and Mills presumably didn't want to burn any political capital. Congressional Research Service (CRS) reports show that the State Department simply allocated $2.5 million a year from its own Economic Support Funds toward the IFI. CRS also reports that since fiscal year 2014, the Obama administration had not requested funds for the IFI. The Trump administration does not include IFI funding in its budgets. (Years later, in conversation with Conor O'Clery, O'Leary said about the IFI, "The Americans would like to withdraw but each year they try to withdraw, I go to Senator Leahy ... and the money will come through again. And when Hillary Clinton is elected, we should be in very good shape.")

On March 17, 2011, *Irish Times* journalist Lara Marlowe reported that "the House of Representatives withdrew funding for the International Fund for Ireland." Marlowe claimed that Obama administration officials and Congress were "furious" about this, yet, oddly, she was unable to provide any names. Marlowe claimed that I was one of three individuals who had "led the campaign to dismantle the IFI." (The other two were a Republican congressman, Jason Chaffetz, and right-wing radio presenter Glenn Beck—the same two people O'Leary would reference.) She also wrote that I wanted those funds spent on the Mitchell Scholarship "instead."

Marlowe neglected to mention the very important fact that we sought funding for the Mitchell *after* the IFI said it wasn't seeking any further funding. How could I therefore "lead the campaign to dismantle" something they said they were dismantling themselves? Furthermore, all indications from Capitol Hill were that it was ending contributions to the IFI. To suggest I *caused* that to happen is to suggest I have a lot more time and influence than I do. As the IFI funding was being eliminated, it made perfect sense for us to seek funding for the Mitchell.

Marlowe also unquestioningly relayed the recurring, tiresome suggestion that there was "a danger of regression" in Northern Ireland. But there was absolutely no evidence to back up the suggestion that somehow, without a few million dollars of US funding, Northern Ireland would return to violence.

In writing her story, Marlowe never bothered to ring me for a comment. When I ran into her that night at the St. Patrick's Day party at the White House, I asked why she hadn't included the very significant fact that the IFI had previously said it didn't want the money anymore. She told me she hadn't known that. I asked her if she knew anything about the IFI or if she'd even taken a look at an annual report. Her response to both was "no."

I ceased to be invited to embassy functions and saw a change in the Irish consulates in the US. A few months later, when we planned an event in Chicago that would bring positive attention to the universities in Ireland and Northern Ireland, I naturally reached out to Martin Rouine, the Irish consul general. We had never met, but he received all the email updates on the US-Ireland Alliance, and a year earlier, when he learned we might do something in Chicago, he offered to be helpful. But when I followed up after the fallout with Collins, Rouine feigned he'd never heard of our organization and, in a hostile tone, asked what I was doing on his "patch." I ignored the hostility, stayed on the high road, and offered to invite guests he might wish to have attend our reception with Ruairi Quinn, Ireland's education minister. Sensing he was not going to work with me and concerned that he might even try to sabotage things, I tipped off Minister Quinn that I would not be expecting any help from Rouine in Chicago. Within hours, I got an ass-covering email from Rouine, which was 180 degrees from how he'd spoken to me on the phone, now saying he'd be helpful. That suggested that the minister, or his office, had been in touch. With his email as cover, Rouine quickly disappeared. The Chicago event was a huge success, without the help of the consulate.

The chill was felt again when a new consul general to New York City arrived. Noel Kilkenny had been in the embassy in Washington years earlier, and we had a friendly relationship.

Just after he arrived at his new post, I met him in his office in New York. What I thought would be a half-hour meeting stretched for hours, all positive, picking up where we left off years earlier. Noel mentioned someone who would be helpful to the Alliance and promised to get me the details. He also offered—I hadn't asked—to have the Mitchells to his home for a reception. Despite several efforts on my part to follow up after, Noel went silent for a long time. It was as if someone had marked his card.

Special Envoy

Like funding for the International Fund for Ireland, special envoys had outlived their usefulness; but also like the IFI, some would keep asking for them. Again, this begging bowl approach of constantly asking for money and envoys was not going down well with most in the Washington policy establishment who felt there were much bigger issues going on in the world. The US had done its part, and it was time for Northern Ireland's leaders to lead.

The first special envoy for Northern Ireland was Senator George Mitchell back in the 1990s. By the summer of 2008, so much progress had been made that it was hard to see what purpose another special envoy would serve.

In a book published during the 2008 campaign, former US secretary of state Madeleine Albright wrote about the positive role Senator Mitchell played as President Clinton's special envoy to Northern Ireland. But Albright also noted that "such tools can be overused" and should only be used when "the challenge is just too much for conventional diplomacy, or if only a small push is needed to get an important job done." By 2008, neither situation existed in Northern Ireland.

Just before the Democratic convention in Denver in August 2008, the Obama campaign released an Obama fact sheet I wrote on Irish issues. In running it by the campaign staff earlier in the month, I flagged for them that a few Irish Americans would want a special envoy, but neither Tony Lake nor I could make a case that one was necessary at that stage. But just to leave the door open a crack, I wrote that portion of the statement to say that Obama would "consult with the Taoiseach, the British Prime Minister, and party leaders in Northern Ireland to determine whether a special US envoy for Northern Ireland continues to be necessary or whether a senior administration official, serving as point person for Northern Ireland, would be most effective." Hardly earth-shattering stuff.

But Congressmen Joe Crowley and Richie Neal and Maryland governor Martin O'Malley suggested outrage at the Obama position. At the Democratic Convention, Mary Lou Hartman, then the director of our scholarship program, approached O'Malley to introduce herself as someone who went to high school in Baltimore with his sister. Knowing that Mary Lou worked with me and that I was responsible for writing that Obama statement, O'Malley poked his finger in Mary Lou's clavicle with each syllable as he stated, "There Will Be A Spe-cial En-voy!" None of these people offered reasons why there needed to be a special envoy; they simply wanted to demand one. Egos were raw. Crowley, Neal, and O'Malley had all backed Clinton, who had just dropped out of the race in June. In slowly making the switch to Obama, they seemed determined to exact a pound of flesh, never mind how minor the issue.

While in Ireland the next month, I received a call from Denis McDonough, the lead foreign policy adviser on the campaign staff, who would eventually become Obama's chief of staff. Denis was annoyed that Crowley, Neal, and O'Malley were haranguing him, and he wanted me to agree to his walking back on the special envoy issue. In campaigns, there is a tendency to tell people what they want to hear to get them off your back. I told Denis my view hadn't changed, there was no need for an envoy, our statement already said we'd discuss it later, and Denis wasn't going to get me to say otherwise. He told me that he was going to just do it, just make them happy. I told him he could obviously do what he liked, that it was his decision, but it wasn't going to be my advice.

On September 18, the campaign put out a statement: "After consultations with the members of his senior panel of advisers on Irish issues and informal soundings with British and Irish officials, Senator Obama has said that if he becomes president, he will appoint a senior envoy to Ireland who will build on the groundbreaking achievements of the Clinton administration and help bring the historic process to final fruition."

Obama won, Clinton became his secretary of state, and no special envoy was ever named.

But the issue would die a slow death. On March 17, 2009, when Martin McGuinness and Peter Robinson joined Hillary Clinton for a press conference at the State Department, the secretary of state said a special envoy would be appointed: "We waited until we had the opportunity to consult with the leaders of Northern Ireland and of the Republic of Ireland about the best way to structure our relationship going forward." (That was what I wrote in Obama's statement when he was a candidate for president. It was what Denis McDonough later walked back.)

A few days after that press conference, Marion McKeone wrote in the *Sunday Tribune* that "the announcement that a special envoy is being appointed to Northern Ireland seemed to come as news to the Department of State, which is charged with making such appointments. At this point in the peace process, precisely what would a special envoy do? No one at the Department of State seems to know the answer to that one

either. The DOS appeared even more perplexed by First Minister
Peter Robinson's claim that Obama is poised to appoint an official to examine investment opportunities between Northern
Ireland. . . . A separate source suggested . . . that it is extremely
unlikely that a dedicated special envoy of the calibre of Senator
George Mitchell or Richard Haass would be appointed, given
the demands on the Department of State and the paucity of
top-notch candidates who can be dispatched to more urgent
global flashpoints. What is more likely is that 'someone at the
Department of State will be given the Northern Ireland folder
along with a bundle of other folders,' he said."

Months passed. On July 22, Susan Falvella-Garraty wrote
in the *Irish Echo* that "the US State Department was declining
to comment on any appointment." The next day, Niall O'Dowd
claimed that Hillary Clinton herself would be the special envoy,
and that was then repeated in the *Belfast Telegraph*. I was in
San Francisco that week because Irish senator David Norris
was speaking at an Alliance event. Confused by the varying
accounts, I asked someone who would likely know the back-
story of what was going on and was told that when Taoiseach
Bertie Ahern and Shaun Woodward, the British secretary of
state for Northern Ireland, met with Secretary Clinton, and she
was complaining about how long the vetting process took, she
assured them that she was keeping a personal eye on Northern
Ireland. That then was blown out of proportion and morphed
into her *being* the special envoy.

Annoyed at the absurdity of this, State Department spokesperson PJ Crowley told the *Irish Echo*, "She is the Secretary of
State, not a special envoy." Finally, the secretary of state found
it necessary to scupper the nonsense herself, making clear that,
not only would she not be the special envoy; there wouldn't
be one. The *Belfast Telegraph* reported on July 31, 2009, that
she said in a BBC interview that she didn't "see the need for

someone fulltime." She rightly noted, "This is not the 1990s. George Mitchell did his job and did it very well."

In September 2009, Clinton named Declan Kelly as her "economic" envoy for Northern Ireland, which was seen by many as an easy sop to one of her campaign fund-raisers. Kelly was an Irish-born, New York–based public relations man who would end up doing damage to the Clintons with a company he later created called Teneo.

There was no need for an economic envoy, and Kelly's tenure yielded little. Making a case for US corporate investment in Northern Ireland had been difficult from the start. Any advantage Northern Ireland may have by being part of the United Kingdom is offset by its geographical distance from London. And most US investment was attracted to Ireland's much lower corporate tax rate.

Compounding the inherent difficulties, Kelly was making his pitch during an economic recession in the US. In October 2010, Kelly had Secretary Clinton host an event intended to bring together potential US investors with Northern Ireland political leaders. But at the time, Northern Ireland's unemployment rate hovered around 7 percent while the US rate was 3 percent higher on average, and in several states, much higher. The event received little attention at the time. The State Department probably did not want to highlight the fact that it was encouraging US companies to send jobs overseas. Would the Irish or British governments host a conference to steer investment from their countries to the US?

In May 2011, Declan Kelly resigned. That was two months after I questioned, in the Northern Ireland journal *The Detail*, why the US government even had an economic envoy. Kelly finally told an audience in Northern Ireland that they needed to invest in themselves.

While the immediate response from some in Northern Ireland was the usual call for another envoy, some were prepared to advocate for themselves. In the *Belfast Telegraph*, Northern Ireland Chamber of Commerce CEO Ann McGregor was quoted as saying, "The Northern Ireland Chamber believes that a bold economic statement is required and nothing signifies our 'can-do' approach more than the immediate appointment of a Northern Ireland economic ambassador to the US." Northern Ireland needs more of that confidence and less of the old culture of dependency.

Again, when Stella O'Leary spoke in 2015 at the Clinton Institute for American Studies at University College Dublin with Conor O'Clery, O'Clery listed a series of envoys that followed after Senator Mitchell and questioned whether there was any continued need for a special envoy. O'Leary floundered and then said, "At the moment symbolically to have some connection . . . whether it's an envoy or some other way. . . . The Americans have a large investment there now, not just in the terms of the amount of money they give to the Fund but also in terms of President Clinton's and George Mitchell's connection." She went on to mention a Clinton international summer school she said she established in Derry, then continued, "And there's the Mitchell Scholarship." She also said, "I'm sure if Hillary Clinton were President that she would like to maintain that connection." Stella was all over the place and suggested she and Secretary Clinton supported the Mitchell Scholarship. But Capitol Hill staffers told me that Stella called to urge them not to support the Mitchell Scholarship program, and it was Secretary Clinton's State Department that eliminated funding for the Mitchell Scholarship in February 2012. It's unclear whether the Mitchell could have received the endowment funding we were seeking, but we certainly would have had a better chance if the Irish ambassador, Balderston, and others had not been so intent on making sure that didn't happen.

Once Trump became president, those who regularly called for a special envoy—the words are like a mantra—were doing so again. In September 2017, Congressman Richie Neal said he'd met with President Trump and got him to promise a special envoy.

In February 2018, Rex Tillerson, secretary of state, was reportedly considering names for a special envoy, but it always sounded pretty iffy. History shows that chatter about a special envoy ticks up when an Irish politician visits, and then it quickly fades.

President Trump unceremoniously fired Tillerson on March 13, 2018, just days before Taoiseach Varadkar met with President Trump in the White House.

Varadkar has consistently sent the signal, rightly in my opinion, that an envoy isn't needed.

While the new Sinn Fein leader, Mary Lou McDonald, said she felt an envoy could be helpful, I'm perplexed about why she thinks a representative of Trump (who is a fan of Brexit) would help the situation.

What Senator Mitchell did in the mid-1990s was critical and necessary, but what's needed now are for the leaders there to just lead.

More on Declan Kelly

I met Declan Kelly in Manhattan in 2003, at the suggestion of Niall O'Dowd (who was on our advisory board at the time). Kelly (the brother of Irish Labour TD, Alan Kelly) then headed up a company called Financial Dynamics. It was the only time we met, and I immediately had a bad feeling about him. Despite my personal hesitations, I did the requisite follow-up, given O'Dowd's strong endorsement, but I felt that Kelly was a big talker, and I doubted anything would come of it. Fortunately, it didn't.

Along with O'Dowd, Kelly was heavily involved in a Dublin fund-raiser for Hillary Clinton at the Raglan Road home of Linda O'Shea-Farren in November 2007. Kelly emailed people that tickets would be €1,500 per person, and the funds could be raised only from Americans or Green Card holders. It was reported that $300,000 was expected to be raised. I doubted that Ireland had enough people who were allowed to give in order to raise that kind of money. On November 19, someone was quoted in an *Irish Times* article by Mary Fitzgerald as saying, "The place was awash with Paddies. . . . You were left wondering where were all the Yanks."

A look at the Federal Election Commission's data on fund-raising for Clinton during the 2007–2008 cycle suggests that $55,700 was raised from Americans residing in Ireland—during the entire two-year period, that is, and it's unlikely all of it was related to that particular fund-raiser. Information in the FEC reports seems insufficient to shed light on how much was raised at that fund-raiser and who donated.

In 2008, I recommended that the Obama campaign steer clear of Kelly. It struck me that his only interest was his own business, and I said that he was a negative story waiting to happen.

As more about Kelly has come to light in recent years, the happier I am that the Alliance never became involved with him. In 2014, an Amy Chozick *New York Times Magazine* piece called "Planet Hillary" placed Declan Kelly in the Clinton orbit of "poseurs."

There are several reports about conflicts of interest after Clinton named Kelly to the State Department role. In April 2016, *Politico* reported that long before Kelly left State, he was working on his next project, Teneo Holdings. Rachael Bade reported that Kelly was simultaneously Clinton's special envoy and working for the Clintons as a private consultant. She noted, "Kelly and Doug Band, a close aide to former President

Bill Clinton, were preparing to launch a global consulting business" that would "employ numerous Hillary Clinton associates, including her closest confidante, Huma Abedin, and, for a time, Bill Clinton as 'honorary chairman,' giving clients rare access to the couple and their network of world leaders." Both the *New York Times* and the *New Republic* had previously reported on Teneo's tangled web of relationships, which involved the former president and the Clinton Global Initiative.

Senator Chuck Grassley, chairman of the US Senate Judiciary Committee, was investigating Abedin's employment with Teneo at the same time that she was Clinton's right hand in the State Department. The heat also became such that Bill Clinton had to step down from his role with Teneo.

Negativity . . . pervades this country. We seem to be against so much more than we are for. . . .

Merit is downplayed and mediocrity is excused. There is a spirit of "twill do" rather than "can do."

—Cathal Guiomard, *The Irish Disease and How to Cure It*

Chapter 7

MEDIOCRITY & BEGRUDGERY

The Irish Film Board—Lights, Camera, Inaction

In the last scene of *Star Wars: The Force Awakens*, Rey finds Luke Skywalker at the first Jedi temple. Director J.J. Abrams shot that breathtaking scene on Skellig Michael, off the west coast of Ireland. Those few minutes will mean more tourism for Ireland than *The Quiet Man, Ryan's Daughter,* and all the one-off events, like "the Gathering" and football games combined. And it will bring a new generation of tourists. But it nearly didn't happen. For years, I'd been encouraging J.J. to film in Ireland. The Irish Film Board (IFB) had no interest until it had no choice.

Since 2006, the US-Ireland Alliance has held an annual event in Los Angeles to bring together Irish and Americans in the entertainment fields with the aim of sparking creative collaborations. The Oscar Wilde Awards immediately became one of the hottest tickets in Hollywood during Oscars week.

The idea for the name of the event was the brainchild of Dublin PR man Paul Hayes. Paul originally suggested calling it Oscars Wilde (given that the event is held just days before those other Oscars are presented), but our lawyers thought the Academy of Motion Picture Arts and Sciences might object. I thought they might not if we sought their permission, but we ultimately decided to take the path of least resistance and name it (without the *s*) for the Irish writer who made celebrity an art form.

The event brings out studio executives, writers, directors, producers, Oscar nominees, and many others. Some of those who have been honored, participated, or just attended include Jim Sheridan, Neil Jordan, Steven Spielberg, Kathleen Kennedy, Al Pacino, Jodie Foster, Hylda Queally, Kate Winslet, Marion Cotillard, Saoirse Ronan, Lenny Abrahamson, Sarah Greene, Terry George, John Logan, Colm Meaney, Seamus McGarvey, Fiona Shaw, Jim Brooks, Anjelica Huston, Cecelia Ahern, Charlize Theron, Ruth Negga, Dana Delany, Colin Farrell, Stephen Colbert, Conan O'Brien, James Corden, Benedict Cumberbatch, Idris Elba, and Orlando Bloom. We've also used the event to recognize the Irish who are nominated for Academy Awards.

A concert is part of the night's activities, and these have included performances by Van Morrison, Glen Hansard, and Snow Patrol, to name a few.

The event is intentionally small—around 450 guests—so people can meet. It is not a boozy hooley, and not every aspiring actor or every person with an Irish surname in Los Angeles is invited. It is decidedly not a one-thousand-people-in-a-ball-room, black-tie dinner. Part of the reason guests return is because it is more like a house party. There is no VIP room, and the speaking program is kept short. We encourage guests to wear jeans.

For the last several years, the event has been held at Bad Robot, the Santa Monica production company of J.J. Abrams. J.J. is the creator of numerous television shows, including *Lost* and *Alias*. He directed and produces the current group of Star Wars films, and his company is behind the Star Trek and Mission Impossible franchises. J.J.'s wife, and co-CEO of the company, Katie McGrath, is an old friend going back twenty-five years, when we both worked for Senator Kennedy. Bad Robot is a treat for guests who enjoy J.J.'s menagerie of toys and printing presses. There is an outdoor courtyard where the concert happens and a rooftop deck where we present the awards. As an added bonus, J.J. usually emcees and is very funny. I love working with Katie and J.J. because they're positive; they just get stuff done and aren't interested in drama (in the behavior sense as opposed to the genre).

The Oscar Wilde Awards grew out of the golf tournament the Alliance regularly held in Ireland before the 2008 economic crash. The tournament brought together senior business executives from the US to play with their Irish counterparts, again with the aim of building ties between our countries. In 2003, Naoise Barry of the Irish Film Board knew that Dick Cook, the then chairman of Walt Disney Studios, was playing in our tournament. Naoise told me that Irish film producer Morgan O'Sullivan had been making films for Disney for years but had never met Cook. Morgan was an associate producer on the film *Veronica Guerin*, starring Cate Blanchett. The film was about the courageous Irish journalist who was murdered because of her relentless pursuit of drug lords in Dublin. The film was soon to be released and distributed by a Disney company, and Dick brought the film with him to Ireland and screened it for us at the Liffey Valley Shopping Centre in the Dublin suburbs. Naoise asked if I would arrange for Morgan to meet Dick and have a photo taken, which we did at the tournament's concluding dinner at Trinity College. It was then that I realized that many in the film industry in Ireland didn't know many of their counterparts in Los Angeles. When I explained to Jim Sheridan and Neil Jordan the idea for an event in LA that would do that, they kindly and quickly agreed to be the first honorees. In addition to honoring Ireland's most successful directors, the third honoree for the first event was David Holmes, the Belfast DJ who was behind the music of many Steven Soderbergh films, including *Ocean's Eleven.*

Unfortunately, the Irish state agencies were less than enthusiastic about an idea that was not their own. It was another example of all too common petty, bureaucratic, civil service behavior. My experiences are not unlike those described by Paddy Cosgrave when he announced in 2015 why he was moving his Web Summit from Dublin to Lisbon—no joined-up thinking and more begrudgery than support. With state agencies, it is often about owning or killing something rather than partnering and supporting.

Naoise was initially enthusiastic, or so I thought. He told me the Irish Film Board liked the idea of the LA event, but the funding decision wasn't up to them. I would need the support of John O'Donoghue, Ireland's minister for arts in 2005. O'Donoghue and I would both be in County Kerry in June, and we agreed to meet at the Park Kenmare, a lovely hotel in a small picturesque town of the same name. O'Donoghue, like the then minister for enterprise, Micheál Martin, immediately saw the potential for the event and promised support. Naoise was surprised when I quickly came back to say that O'Donoghue had committed $50,000 from Tourism Ireland and the same from the Irish Film Board. Minister Martin committed Enterprise Ireland to $50,000. I thought Naoise would be thrilled, as he had told me I just needed O'Donoghue's support. Instead, he told me that just because the minister said they'd support didn't mean the IFB necessarily would. (If you're scratching your head, welcome to my world.)

I also quickly learned that some at Enterprise Ireland were not happy that their minister, the person who was elected to actually make decisions, made one. Two people in Ireland relayed to me virtually the same sentence in terms of what different Enterprise Ireland officials were saying: "This is a great idea; it should have been our idea; let's let it die, and we'll steal it from her." That explained why Enterprise Ireland's LA office hadn't lifted a finger to make the most of the event by inviting clients, arranging meetings around the event, etc. It wasn't until Minister Martin unexpectedly decided to attend that they hurriedly had to pull the finger out and create some deliverables for him. Clearly the plan had been to make no effort in hopes that the event would fail and then they could report back that it wasn't of any real value. The Tourism Ireland representatives were mainly fixated on our reserving a table for the head of their US office—never mind that there were no reserved tables for anyone; their man had to have one.

The first year doing any event is often the most difficult, and this was no exception. While we were just trying to nail down the logistics, people started coming out of the woodwork demanding tickets, without wanting to pay for them, of course. The women who run the Irish Film and Television Academy Awards (IFTAs) were incessant. The IFTAs is an annual awards dinner in Ireland, which the Irish Film Board supported despite annual bad press about the repeated logistical failures. A little-known Irish actor in LA sent me blistering emails about how his relative worked in the Department of Finance, and he would see to it that the Mitchell Scholarship wasn't funded if he wasn't invited. We also had to deal with the honorary Irish consul general in Los Angeles, Finbar Hill. Honorary consul general is a title the Department of Foreign Affairs bestows on Irish individuals in cities where there is no official Irish government representation. In exchange for the title, they help out the real diplomats on what are usually minor things. Hill provided not a bit of assistance to the event but, like Tourism Ireland with the reserved table, had all sorts of demands, including a reserved parking spot (there were no reserved parking spots; it was all valet). Later, Hill told me that I should "pay him due deference." The Irish civil servants and Hill were higher maintenance than any of the actual talent. Julia Roberts didn't ask for reserved parking, nor did Tom Cruise. Jodie Foster drove up in her Prius, no entourage, no demands, just gracious participation. I'm reminded of something that the late John Burke, the former head of protocol in the Irish Department of Foreign Affairs, said about those who demand tickets and seats at the "right" table: "Those who matter don't care and those who care don't matter." Despite state agency begrudgery, the event has been a success for more than a decade and has led to collaborations among artists, and business for both countries.

On more than one occasion, we've made someone an "honorary" Irishman or Irishwoman. J.J. Abrams, Paul Rudd, Michelle Williams, and James Corden have all participated in this bit of fun. Our first honorary Irishman was James. L. Brooks.

Lou Pitt is a Hollywood agent I first met when he played in our golf tournament in Ireland. At various times, Lou was the agent for Christopher Plummer and Arnold Schwarzenegger. We stayed in touch after the golf tournament, and Lou attended our Hollywood event and even contributed to it, despite not being Irish. It was Lou who told me that Jim Brooks loved Ireland and suggested we find a way to honor him. Jim is the creator of *The Simpsons*. He also won the Oscar for directing *Terms of Endearment*, which also won the Oscar for best picture. His other Oscar-nominated films include *As Good as It Gets*, *Jerry Maguire*, and *Broadcast News*. While I was delighted when Jim agreed to be honored, the Irish Film Board was underwhelmed. Naoise Barry responded, "But he's not

Irish." I had explained that one of our objectives was to get people into the room who might make films in Ireland and that we should be expansive about whom we honor. Someone like Jim also draws others in Hollywood to the event, and all these people were there for the Film Board to meet and follow up with later. The speeches made by the honorary Irish are often the funniest or the most poignant. Jim told a hysterical story of long believing he was Irish before realizing he was actually Jewish. Paul Rudd talked about his father, an expert on the *Titanic* who loved Cobh, the seaside town in Ireland that was the last port of call for the *Titanic*. It turned out that our event fell on the birthday of Paul's father, who had died that year. There weren't many dry eyes in the room when Paul spoke of scattering his father's ashes in Ireland. J.J. brought the house down with his story of losing his wallet in Ireland and how the policewoman who was to return it to him demanded he first tell her how *Lost* would end (it was the year of the final season of the popular television show).

Sometimes even the Irish aren't Irish enough for the Film Board. The same year we honored Brooks, we honored actress Fiona Shaw, who was born and raised in Cork. The award-winning theater actress, whose Medea was the most memorable performance I have ever seen on Broadway, is also known to countless Harry Potter fans for her portrayal of Harry's awful Muggle aunt Petunia. But when I informed the Film Board we would be honoring Fiona, the silence was deafening. They had to tread more carefully here because Fiona actually is Irish, but I got the strong impression that they felt that she wasn't Irish enough since she lives in London and works mainly there. The Irish can be very insular and tribal, and whether or not one counts as Irish is ever-changing, depending on the context and if they want something from you.

Naoise also didn't like our decision to honor Northern Ireland–born Van Morrison—he didn't think anyone would be interested. That was just daft. Who wouldn't want to see Van Morrison perform in a small venue? The IFB seemed intent on narrowly defining the event. Many of Morrison's songs were used in films, but the Film Board didn't seem to value the contribution of music to films the same way they valued the more obvious, like actors, writers, and directors.

After being honored at our event, Jim Brooks created an episode of *The Simpsons* about closing an Irish pub. In what was a first, he personally took the episode to Dublin to premiere it, and Twentieth Century Fox told me they spent well over $100,000 related to that trip and the premiere. The episode featured his co-honoree from our event, Colm Meaney, and Glen Hansard and Marketa Irglova, who sang on the night. Fiona Shaw, who was honored along with Brooks and Meaney, saw Duke Special perform that evening. That led to the Belfast singer-songwriter joining Fiona in the cast of *Mother Courage and Her Children* at the National Theatre of London. Speaking of his participation at our event, Duke Special later said, "The whole direction of my career changed that night."

Two Irish singers, Paddy Casey and SJ McArdle, received recording contracts with Sony after performing at our first event; another found a manager. Laura Livingstone, a woman from Northern Ireland who was working in visual effects on the US West Coast, met with J.J.'s team at Bad Robot after the event, an encounter that resulted in her company first working on an app for Bad Robot and, later, doing visual effects work on *Star Trek*. Screenwriter Conor Ryan found his agents and collaborators because of the Oscar Wilde Awards. There are numerous examples of others who have benefited in similar ways.

In recent years, there had not been much in the way of big Hollywood productions in Ireland. The last one was *King Arthur* in 2003, with about €45 million spent in Ireland on production. Indigenous producers have done well and are to be congratulated for securing and originating television shows like *Camelot, The Tudors, Vikings,* and *Penny Dreadful.* But the opportunity exists for Ireland to play a much larger role in international film production and to even secure tentpoles (the blockbuster films), which bring jobs, significant spend in the country, and tourism. Knowing this, I steered several Hollywood producers to the Irish Film Board, assuming this would be welcomed. More often than not, they didn't follow up, and when they did, they did so inadequately. It was as if they didn't want the business, and I came to blows with the IFB more than once over this.

In LA, I had lunch with Jim Brooks and Lou Pitt at the Hotel Bel-Air. Brooks was effusive about Ireland, and I encouraged the IFB to follow up with him in hopes of getting him to make a film in Ireland. Part of the Film Board's problem was not having proper representation in Los Angeles. They had a young man, named Jonathan Loughran, who had worked for Enterprise Ireland and then for the IFB. Naoise Barry described him to me as an assistant to set up his meetings for his trips to LA, trips that were infrequent. Loughran's idea of following up seemed to amount to sending an email, and if he got no response, that was that. I asked Brooks if I could give his personal email address to Simon Perry, the then CEO of the IFB, thinking Perry would make more of an effort than Loughran. Perry too dropped the ball. For one thing, he made no secret of his disdain for big Hollywood productions. He was more interested in indie films and Europe, and he didn't care that the production of a wide variety of films could be complementary and beneficial to those who worked in film in Ireland. Perry also begrudged our event being such a success. When I met with him once in the Westbury Hotel in Dublin and asked why they weren't following up on leads, he said, "It's *your* event." As I said to him, who cares? Most guests hadn't a clue whose event it was. The Irish civil servants seemed hell-bent on wanting nothing to come from it.

Even though Jim Brooks stayed late into the night when he was honored, and was totally accessible, Perry never bothered to introduce himself. It took him nine months to follow up with Brooks. People in Hollywood need to get things done on a schedule. Time literally is money. When the Irish Film Board takes months to follow up, producers understandably assume that it takes a long time to get things done in Ireland. I complained to Niall O Donnchu, the assistant secretary in the Department of Arts, and he did raise the matter with Perry, which was what probably eventually caused Perry to email Brooks and feign interest. Perry's unimpressive "pitch" to Jim amounted to, "If you ever want to make a movie in Ireland, let us know." This seemed to be as much of an effort as the Film Board wanted to make in Hollywood, and I would learn that lesson time and again.

Underlying all of this is accountability. The Irish Film Board (recently renamed Screen Ireland) has a budget from the state, and they are paid regardless of whether they bring big productions to Ireland. There are no incentives to deliver.

Despite my experiences with Barry, Loughran, and Perry, I still wanted to help on the production front. Ireland had been through the 2008 economic crash, so the jobs were needed, and there are so many talented, creative people in the film and entertainment space in Ireland. I wasn't prepared to give up so easily. A small golden circle was preventing greater opportunities, and those losing out often had no way to challenge the status quo.

In 2010, I asked J.J. Abrams if he would meet with the chairman of the Irish Film Board, James Morris. J.J. agreed and on the day spent more than an hour with us at his Santa Monica office and brought in several members of his team. Knowing that Morris wasn't himself a producer, I invited Irish producer

Alan Moloney to the meeting because I expected he could talk the talk with J.J. and his team. Before that March meeting, I was annoyed when the only thing Morris raised with me in advance was his desire to talk to J.J. about his own editing company, Windmill Lane. I told him that was not on—I had arranged this meeting for him as the head of the Irish Film Board to pitch the country, not so he could pitch his own private business. Conflict of interest is a recurrent theme when it comes to the Irish Film Board.

I was happy Moloney had participated, because he could answer many of the practical questions J.J. and his team had. I was surprised that Morris didn't bring anything to leave behind, such as the information on the tax benefits of filming in Ireland.

Not long after that meeting, I emailed Morris to suggest steps for following up with J.J. Given that the IFB had never adequately followed up with Jim Brooks, I copied the email to several people, including Taoiseach Brian Cowen, Minister Martin Mansergh (who had attended the event), and Niall O Donnchu. I knew Morris would hate that I copied the others, but I'd learned my lesson. The initial steps I suggested would be less than a half day's work. I suggested that the next minister for the arts (it would soon be Mary Hanafin) follow up. J.J.'s office told me the IFB never reached out. They clearly didn't want the business, and no one higher up in the food chain cared enough to demand results.

I ran into Morris a couple of months later in Dublin. It was late May 2010, and I distinctly remember the moment, as we were both at an event that Riverdance producer John McColgan was holding at Dublin Castle, once the seat of Britain's administration of Ireland. While walking down a wide, grand staircase, I spotted Morris, who was with his colleague, Teresa McGrane. I asked, "James, how come you never followed up with J.J. Abrams?" He said that he'd been "busy with the day job," but he guessed he would send him an email because "late is better than never." I minced no words in telling him that it wasn't. I could see McGrane sense the tension and hang back to stay out of that conversation. I told Morris he could be assured that numerous US states and countries around the world would kill for such a meeting with Abrams and would have wasted no time in following up. Blasé about my finding his response dissatisfying, Morris concluded with, "They know where we are if they want to make a movie here." It was Simon Perry's response all over again.

I still cannot understand this. The Irish Film Board is meant to be luring productions to Ireland. I asked several Irish friends at the time what I might be missing. Is this something Irish? Is it cultural? Is it a fear that they'll fail to get the business, so why bother to try? Is it a fear that they will get the business, but that would then mean they'd actually have to work? One Irish friend told me that, as an American, I would assume that if Morris brought in a big film production, he'd be applauded for a job well done, but he'd as likely be viewed by many Irish as "losing the run of himself."

In February 2011, McGrane informed me that Morris wouldn't be attending the next event because he was busy. I complained to Niall O Donnchu, Ireland's assistant secretary in the Department of Arts, about the lack of significant Film Board representation to work the room and about how the Irish Film Board repeatedly failed to follow up on leads that resulted from our event. O Donnchu wrote to me, saying, "Maybe you shouldn't be so unceasingly snippy about your main sponsor." Given the state of the Irish economy at the time, O Donnchu should have been snippy with his colleagues who failed to make the most they could of this event. Some senior civil servants tend to forget that it's not their money but the taxpayers' money. (It was much like Ambassador Collins's view that the use of the Irish embassy was his to give or withhold.) Within months of receiving that email, Culture Ireland and the Irish Film Board went from providing $150,000 for the Oscar Wilde Awards to zero.

Within two months of the email from O Donnchu, we made our application to Culture Ireland for funding for the event for the next year. We applied well before the May deadline. According to Culture Ireland's own website, a decision would be made in June (historically, Culture Ireland and the IFB coordinated and replied to us at the same time). We never received a response to our application from Culture Ireland.

Simon Perry's five-year stint as CEO of the Film Board ended in January 2011. In February, it was announced that entertainment lawyer James Hickey would become the next CEO. In March, there were changes in Taoiseach Enda Kenny's Cabinet, and Jimmy Deenihan became the minister of culture. I knew Jimmy slightly, as he generously helped when I took a class of Mitchell Scholars to Listowel Writers' Week, which is in his constituency. Jimmy is a nice man but was no match for conniving bureaucrats adept at running circles around ministers. And Cabinet reshuffles are good times for civil servants who want to mess. Because Hickey was new to the job, he seemed to leave the decisions about our funding to Chairman James Morris, who was not happy I had complained that he hadn't followed up with Abrams.

The funding issue played out over the summer of 2011. By late July, long after we were due a response from Culture Ireland, I told the IFB and Culture Ireland that we needed their response. I copied Deenihan on my emails in hopes that the civil servants would have to behave in an aboveboard manner if a minister might be watching. On August 3, O Donnchu informed me that the IFB would be responding.

What none of them knew at the time—not O Donnchu, not Eugene Downes, the head of Culture Ireland, not the IFB— was that a sympathetic civil servant had tipped me off that they had already taken a decision not to fund, but they wanted to teach me a lesson, and as they couldn't explain *why* they wouldn't fund the successful event that was clearly beneficial for Ireland, their plan was to just never respond to our request. This tip turned out to be accurate.

Knowing the decision had already been made and we were just being messed about, on August 9, I withdrew the request. What is interesting in hindsight was the way Morris was playing us after the decision had been made. The officials were caught off guard when we withdrew our request. On that very day, Morris wrote to me (I think our emails crossed in the ether) asking for details never requested before. Remember, the applications had been made months ago, and this event had been happening, successfully, for years. I took that last email from Morris to be an ass-covering exercise so they could later claim they were considering this when we walked.

I later put in a Freedom of Information request with the Department of Arts. As we had never received a response to our application, I wanted to see what I could learn. What was provided proved what I knew. On July 9, the Irish Film Board had a meeting and decided against funding. We were never informed of that decision. Those notes of the board meeting say only that our event was discussed, and it was agreed not to fund. There was no explanation anywhere of the discussion, who said what, who voted how, and most important, what was the basis for the decision. The event had been massively successful, and we had just announced at the end of June that we were moving the event to J.J. and Katie's Bad Robot. That should have been a major plus, as far as the Film Board was concerned. Furthermore, there was a recent major review of the audiovisual sector in Ireland, and our event perfectly coincided with the stated goals of the industry in Ireland.

When Paddy Cosgrave moved the Web Summit to Lisbon, and Irish state agencies argued that they had been supportive,

Cosgrave used the phrase "hush money"—they weren't giving as much as they should or could but were giving just enough that it would be expected that he'd be grateful and keep his mouth shut. In our case, the state agencies had been giving money, and I was to just be grateful but not actually expect them to follow up and make something of it for the country.

Even more interestingly, it appears there was never a Culture Ireland board meeting on our application, as is required. For all the talk of Culture Ireland's supposed independent status, it was just another entity that O Donnchu ultimately controlled. Despite my request for board meeting notes from the beginning of January 2011, the only meeting appears to have occurred late in September and only mentions that we withdrew our request. So, who exactly made the decision not to fund, and why is there no record of the required board meeting?

Also interesting was an email that did turn up in the FOI request, an email from McGrane at the IFB to Eugene Downes at Culture Ireland. The email, dated June 30, said: "You will probably have seen this from Trina re 2012 venue for Oscar Wilde? She appears to be taking 2012 funding for granted. I guess the sooner we can finalise a joint decision and communicate to her, the better." Further suggestion that the decision had been made even before the Irish Film Board met. (I never heard from Downes again after the 2011 event—no reference, ever, to our application or its being unofficially rejected.)

Also, in the Freedom of Information packet from Culture Ireland was a list of five negative newspaper articles about me and the Alliance that were tagged for the minister's office. Four out of five were from Niall O'Dowd's tabloids. The other was a story going back to 2008, when Irish actress Fionnula Flanagan declined to be honored at our event because she didn't like my opinion piece on the illegal immigration issue. What was not there was any reference by Culture Ireland to the thousands of positive press clips (clips we regularly provided to them). It was as if, after we had withdrawn the funding request, someone was trying to create a case for it being just as well that they weren't sponsoring.

While every year there was an unnecessary level of frustration that accompanied Irish state agencies, we had no such problems with other sponsors. I don't know if it's malevolence, incompetence, or a combination of both, but despite a then six-year track record, the Irish state agencies never embraced the opportunity.

When it became public knowledge that we withdrew our request, Morris began to spin. He confirmed that we withdrew our request and cutely suggested that given the state of the economy, wasn't it great that we could do the event without their money. He made no reference to the fact that they had decided against funding without telling us and that it had nothing to do with the Irish economy.

Sexism is often hard to know or prove, and I'm always slow to come to such a conclusion, but I can't help but feel that was part of it. It was O Donnchu who used the word "snippy." Did he ever use that word with a man? A male friend in the Irish civil service said it was a word O Donnchu would use only for women and gay men. James Morris said I was "aggressive." Downes was annoyed when the Irish Arts Council, independently, contributed to our event. He tried to keep them from funding by telling them that I was "difficult." In February 2016, according to a State Department memo, an unnamed Irish embassy official described me as "assertive," and used the word negatively.

There is a bigger cultural issue of some men simply not listening to women. On February 7, 2016, on Marian Finucane's Sunday morning radio program, Eamon Dunphy talked about how, in 2005, a woman in the Department of Finance wrote a paper warning about the impending financial crisis, and she was punished by the system. He said another woman in the Central Bank had also warned about the crisis. On an even more important matter, Brooksley Born, the head of the Commodity Futures Trading Commission in the US, warned of the impending disaster if derivatives went unregulated; Alan Greenspan, Larry Summers, and Robert Rubin ignored her. On an episode of *Frontline* for PBS, Arthur Levitt, former chairman of the Securities and Exchange Commission, said, "I didn't know Brooksley Born. I was told that she was irascible, difficult, stubborn, unreasonable." We're still paying the price because she wasn't listened to.

The 2012 event was great despite the Irish state agencies. In attendance were Abrams, Steven Spielberg, Dick Cook, the former head of Disney Studios I first took to Ireland years earlier, and execs from HBO, Disney, and Focus Features, to name just a few. All were people the IFB could have been meeting. Oscar Wilde would have said these civil servants knew the cost of everything and the value of nothing.

Through the years, people in the US have been more than responsive and supportive, including the Irish who have made the US their home. J.J. and Katie graciously offered us the use of Bad Robot for the event. Una Fox, a Disney exec from Dundalk, and Hylda Queally, a County Clare–born agent of many of the world's top actresses, joined our advisory board. Michael Burns, Lionsgate vice chairman, and Garrett Kelleher of Lightstream, made introductions. Des Carey, Cecelia Ahern, and Dana Delany have been among the sponsors. Joanne McGrath and Garret Daly of Mixed Bag Media contributed footage for use at the event. The vast majority of the artists who participate are easy to work with and enjoy the moment, and the Irish who have careers that straddle several countries see the value of the event and embrace it. In receiving his award, cinematographer Seamus McGarvey noted that there "is no nation but the imagination." Colm Meaney hit it on the head the year we honored him when he said, "The broader and the wider we keep our definition of Irishness, and certainly Irish film, then I think the better we will be and the better our work will be."

In the lead-up to our 2013 event, I wondered if it might be time to try again with the Film Board. I was ambivalent. In the summer of 2011, when the new CEO, James Hickey, didn't jump into the conversation about our funding, I found that a bit passive. The word on the street was that, as an attorney who had made his money representing a handful of Ireland's most prolific producers, he would not be that interested in Hollywood because his clients weren't. It took some time for me to fully grasp how negative some Irish producers were about Hollywood productions in Ireland, but more on that later.

Despite a history of experiences that should have held me back, I decided to try again. The most common refrain from my Irish friends was, "Why do you bother?" Many in Ireland are equally disgusted with the way things are, or in this case aren't, done. I had certainly learned my lesson by this stage. But I'm too much of an optimist, or a masochist.

Under the new regime at the IFB, Hickey and Naoise Barry told me they would contribute $15,000 to the event. It was very little in the scheme of things. Friends in Hollywood have noted that any other country would pay for the entire event and be thrilled to have it.

In November 2012, I told J.J. there was a new CEO at the Irish Film Board. I was still embarrassed that Morris had never followed up with him but asked if we might give this one more try. He kindly agreed, and I offered to take Hickey and Barry into Bad Robot just before our event in February 2013. There was talk that the Irish government would have new legislation in place by 2015 to make film production more attractive by increasing tax relief from 28 percent to 32 percent. These approaching changes seemed to make our event somewhat more interesting to the Irish Film Board.

In the meantime, I was leaving nothing to chance. Where the next *Mission Impossible* would be filmed was still up in the air, as the script was still being developed. The Film Board's online presentation of location shots was pretty uninspiring. There were a bunch of stamp-sized images, and you had to click into them individually. I couldn't imagine myself slogging through those, much less expect J.J. and his team to do so. This could surely be done better. Couldn't we make a locations deck that availed of current technology and make it as easy to flip through as reading magazines on an iPad? I spent a lot of time on this, as I wanted to show J.J. and his team all that Ireland had to offer. I watched again the two most recent Mission Impossible films Bad Robot had produced. There were some similar scenes in these films—car chases, scary vertical drops, stately venues for black-tie dinners, underground and street chases, etc. I created a deck with photos thematically arranged. Having traveled to Ireland for more than twenty years, I had many photos myself or knew the photos I wanted. What I didn't have, I asked the IFB for and often went straight to venues to ask for them myself. I emailed the deck to J.J. and his team so they would have an easy-to-view deck in advance of our meeting.

A few months before that meeting, in October 2012, Disney bought Lucasfilm, and Kathleen Kennedy, president of Lucasfilm, was recruiting J.J. to direct what would be called *Star Wars: The Force Awakens*. It would be announced in January that J.J. would direct what became the highest-grossing film of all time in the US, the UK, and Ireland. It was only the third film to gross more than $2 billion worldwide (along with *Titanic* and *Avatar*). By the time we met J.J. and his team in February, both *Mission Impossible* and *Star Wars* were part of the discussion, as were other projects J.J. had in the pipeline. In fact, it was J.J. who mentioned the *Star Wars* possibility.

In December 2012, Barry and Hickey invited me to a gala dinner that would take place in Dublin in late January. Daniel Day Lewis was screening *Lincoln* as a fund-raiser for a hospice in Wicklow, a county Day Lewis called home for many years. The film's director, Steven Spielberg, a regular, quiet visitor to Ireland, would attend. With my own event in LA looming, I couldn't get away, but I was told after that Spielberg met with Taoiseach Enda Kenny and Minister Deenihan. While Spielberg said he didn't have anything in his immediate pipeline that would work for filming in Ireland, he did provide the political leaders with an assessment of Ireland as a place for production, noting that even its newest studio was too small (not high-enough ceilings) for big Hollywood productions.

It was after the Bad Robot meeting in 2013 that I began to see just how resistant some of Ireland's producers were to big international productions. One disincentive was Ireland's unique requirement that foreign companies employ a local production company (not an international norm). For many reasons, some might find it to their advantage to hire a local, but this shouldn't be a requirement. The local producers fought to keep this provision.

Following the Bad Robot meeting, I reached out to the handful of Irish producers who had the capacity to fill this role for a possible large Bad Robot production: Morgan O'Sullivan of World 2000, Alan Moloney of Parallel Films, Andrew Lowe and Ed Guiney of Element Pictures, and Garrett Kelleher of Lightstream Pictures. I asked who might be interested in working with Bad Robot and asked that if they were, would they send me what amounted to a brief paper on their companies that I would share with J.J. Except for Morgan, they all provided their info. Except for Kelleher, no one followed up in the way an American wanting business would.

Ed Guiney told Rebecca Keegan of the *LA Times* in March 2016, "Seeing the Skelligs at the end of 'Star Wars' ... sometimes our politicians run to that rather than the local stuff. We can actually do this here ourselves. We don't need to run to the big shiny American things." Intended or not, it sounds insecure and not exactly welcoming to the community in LA who would have read that comment. On a *Sunday Business Post* podcast in August 2017, Ed talked about wanting to work in other countries, but what if other countries took the same view and didn't welcome Irish producers? We'd be poorer for that.

The one thing Ireland can't do anything about is creative decisions. If a story includes a large cast of Chinese, for example, then Ireland is not going to be the location, regardless of tax incentives. The difficulty at that time with anything like *Mission Impossible* (a big-budget film with at least one major American star) was that the UK's tax incentives were more attractive. Ireland, unlike the UK, did not apply tax incentives to high-priced American actors, like Tom Cruise.

In March 2013, I wrote to Minister Deenihan to suggest a few things that could increase Ireland's chances for luring foreign productions. I raised the issue of tax incentives not applying to non-EU nationals and noted that it can keep out big-budget films. The Film Board told me that there was a willingness in government to address this issue. I had some hope that J.J. might consider filming something in Ireland but feared the slowness of the process could mean Ireland would lose out (it had taken years to sort out the simple legislation on our Mitchell Scholarship). Ireland always seemed to be playing catch-up with the UK on the film-production incentives front.

In October, Deenihan announced that the government would deal with the non-EU talent issue. But what he would come to call "the Tom Cruise clause" wouldn't take effect until 2015. That meant that if *Mission Impossible* hadn't been dinged for creative reasons, Ireland wouldn't have been considered for those tax reasons. Still, it was one step forward.

In November, J.J. clearly had Ireland on his mind when a journalist with the *Scotsman* newspaper interviewed him:

> Ever since the announcement that *Star Wars VII* would begin shooting next year at Pinewood Studios in London, a tug of war has been going on between Trina Vargo, Ireland's film "ambassador" to Hollywood, and Tommy Gormley, the Glaswegian who for the past decade has worked as Abrams' first assistant director, over whose country would best suit the director's vision for exterior shots of a strange alien world—one, presumably, with peaks and glens.
>
> Abrams laughs at the notion of a Celtic civil war that may yet be settled with recourse to lightsabers. "Tommy keeps pushing locations in Scotland and Trina, who is a wonderful Irish woman, keeps pushing locations to shoot in Ireland, so I'm just going to put the two of them in a room and see who comes out, and I'll tell you it's not going to be Tommy. But joking aside, we are looking all over the place for locations and we haven't made that determination yet."

No one was more excited than I was about J.J.'s decision to shoot *Star Wars* in Ireland in the summer of 2014. I knew what just those couple of days of filming on Skellig Michael would mean for jobs for locals and for tourism generally. But it is worth noting that it was only three days of a shoot—meaning Lucasfilm wouldn't require a studio, and they wouldn't need Ireland's tax benefits. It was like a day trip from Pinewood in London, the studio where most of the movie was filmed.

I was repeatedly told by people in the industry in Ireland that larger, local producers can make more money from their own ventures, so they don't want Americans renting the studio space. They can take that position as private businessmen, but the government shouldn't take decisions, or fail to take decisions, that help maintain what amounts to a golden circle of film production. If your job is to do what is best for the nation, and if major US productions can bring in lots of money, provide many jobs, and have the potential to dramatically increase tourism, shouldn't you be supportive of that, in addition to supporting indigenous artists?

Despite the success of the Oscar Wilde event being the catalyst for Abrams's interest in Ireland, in the fall of 2014, the IFB reverted to type. In October, I finally gave up on the IFB after meeting with Barry and Hickey. If they hadn't yet seen the value of this event, they never would. Naoise met me at the door of the Irish Film Board office on Dame Street in Dublin. I was optimistic and excited about how fantastic it was that J.J. had just filmed on Skellig Michael that summer. Naoise's response was to brag about how he didn't have to go down to the set in Kerry; he was away on vacation in France, so Hickey had to go. This was the biggest film opportunity for Ireland in decades, but the point person at the Irish Film Board couldn't be bothered.

Barry spent the two-hour meeting repeatedly telling me, "*Star Wars* coming to Ireland had *nothing* to do with your event." Even Hickey realized Naoise's assertions were off the wall, and he tried to cut him off more than once. It was like some good-cop–bad-cop routine. Both said that the "quality" of the guests at our Oscar Wilde event had "declined" in recent years and that their guests "don't rate it." The years they referred to are the years the event has been held at Bad Robot. If they had no other opportunity than to network with the numerous Bad Robot staff, given the company's large film and television slate, their relatively small contribution would have been money well spent. J.J., Steven Spielberg, Michael Burns (vice chairman of Lionsgate), and Len Amato (president of HBO) had each been at the event two of the previous three years. There were billions of dollars' worth of productions just amongst those four guests. When I pressed them on this issue, they could only complain that two specific Disney execs had not attended recently. I had to point out that they hadn't invited the two individuals! I grew tired of their complaining about the Oscar Wilde event and left, telling them to keep their money. In the last three years, they'd given a total of US $33,000 to the event. Given Tourism Ireland's projected value of *Star Wars* to Ireland, it's a no-brainer.

After the meeting, Naoise sent me an email saying that he wanted to "reiterate" their continued interest in the Oscar Wilde event. I ceased to be surprised by this routine stunt— I've encountered it several times with some civil servants. They say one thing in a meeting or on the phone and then write an ass-covering email after saying something that is completely different. We declined the $20,000 they were offering in sponsorship. Some money is more hassle than it's worth.

Pinewood

In the fall of 2013, Caroline McLaughlin, an Irish woman working for Morgan Stanley in London, asked if she could introduce me to Terry Clune. Caroline and I have worked together for several years on a reception that the US-Ireland Alliance and Morgan Stanley hold annually in London. Clune is the founder and CEO of TaxBack, a tax refund services business. We met at Dunne and Crescenzi, an Italian restaurant on South Frederick Street in Dublin that makes the best espresso anywhere. Clune had initiated a project called ConnectIreland, which was intended to have people use their connections to help create jobs in Ireland. He asked if I would help.

Thinking about what Spielberg and others had said about studio space, I raised the issue with Eoin Egan, an Irishman who worked for Pinewood Studios. Pinewood's base outside of London is where the Harry Potter and James Bond films are made. But Pinewood has expanded over the years with studios in Atlanta, Toronto, and Wales. The company was courted by countries and cities, and they considered opportunities put before them. I wanted to suggest that ConnectIreland work to get Pinewood to set up a studio in Ireland, but I wanted Pinewood's permission to investigate that possibility. I checked with Eoin to make certain that Pinewood wasn't already holding such conversations with the IFB—I had no interest in duplicating efforts. Eoin confirmed that there were no such conversations, and early in 2014, I started the ball rolling. The first thing ConnectIreland had to do was run ideas by the Industrial Development Authority (IDA) to make sure the IDA was not already on the case. The IDA is the Irish state agency tasked with encouraging American multinationals like Medtronic, Pfizer, Apple, Microsoft, Google, and Facebook to set up in Ireland. The IDA initially gave ConnectIreland the green light. I urged ConnectIreland to work with the Irish Film Board, the IDA, and others because this effort would require several state agencies and joined-up thinking. Naoise Barry then told the IDA, which told ConnectIreland, to back off; film was their turf. The IFB, now smelling potential interest from Pinewood, wanted to nudge us out of the picture. I wasn't sure if they just wanted to make this their own or spike it.

Barry had previously told me that the IFB was not talking with Pinewood about establishing a studio in Ireland, that the IFB was not interested in Pinewood's "business model," and that they wouldn't be involved in putting together deals and packages to entice studios to set up in Ireland. Hence my getting personally involved in trying to bridge that, to bring lots of state actors together, to bring jobs to Ireland. I also suggested that they talk with the National Asset Management Agency (NAMA) about property in different parts of Dublin, including Ringsend, as I understood from Pinewood that they would want to be within about a half hour's drive of Dublin and near a creative hub, such as the tech companies based in what has become known as Silicon Docks.

After telling the IDA to back off, the Irish Film Board later issued a request for indications of interest from those (domestic and foreign) interested in building studios. I had just introduced Pinewood as interested, so why not pursue them? This was bureaucratic death by delay. I am all for expansion of the existing studios but there is no need to prevent the possibility of a Pinewood, or any other foreign studio, from setting up. These things are not mutually exclusive. And then, wanting to cover his bases in the event Pinewood did decide to build, Naoise tried to suggest that he was already talking with Pinewood! This was patently false. I anticipated this could happen, hence my asking Eoin if they were talking with the IFB about a studio before I pursued this. It was amusing to hear that Naoise, the longtime IFB employee who was blocking my Pinewood initiative, later went to work, briefly, for Pinewood, and by 2016, he was telling the *Irish Times* that Pinewood was looking to build a studio in Ireland in the next five years. It was also interesting to see that, after the IDA told ConnectIreland to back off, studios were the IFB's turf; in 2016, the IDA went to LA to pitch Hollywood with the IFB. I'm delighted they seem to have taken my advice on joined-up thinking. But that joined-up thinking did not extend to the Oscar Wilde Awards. In December 2015, Barry O'Dowd at the IDA contacted me asking for a free ticket to our event. I instead offered to have the IDA as a sponsor. He replied, "I cannot see how we could get involved." Then the IDA cosponsored a small IFB reception the night before our event. This didn't stop O'Dowd from asking me, two more times, for a free ticket. Now the American Ireland Fund has employed Jonathan Loughran, who was a nuisance when he was at Enterprise Ireland and the Irish Film Board, to hold an event in Los Angeles on the night before our Oscar Wilde Awards. The first order of business is always the split.

The barriers to entry for foreign producers and studios remain when it comes to the film industry in Ireland. Policies over the last several years amount to taking inadequate steps to give the appearance of moving to make Ireland competitive. What has been done is necessary but not sufficient, which explains why Hollywood hasn't rushed in.

The Irish Film Board suggested that increasing the tax incentive to 32 percent would be a game changer. It's not, and that's because 32 percent is technically the rate, but effectively it's more like 26 percent. If a foreign producer wants to make a film in Ireland, he or she is required to have an Irish coproducer to access the tax credit. The only reason that provision exists is so an Irish coproducer can take a percentage of the incentive. The net or real tax incentive means Ireland isn't so attractive. The tax incentive can be paid only to an Irish production company that has been trading for at least twenty-one months. This creates a barrier for a foreign producer to set up a company to make a specific film.

If those obstacles weren't enough, many foreign producers are also excluded because of a rule that says a production company cannot be connected to a broadcaster. This was reportedly established to keep RTE, the state broadcaster, from double dipping on state funding. If you assume that blocking Hollywood was an unintended consequence, it should be easy to fix. But it hasn't been. The only thing the 2015 Irish government budget included regarding film was an increase in the cap on the expenditure eligible for tax relief from €50 million to €70 million. But big productions often have budgets of more than $200 million. That €20 million difference is nothing more than a slight improvement; it would have to be much higher if Ireland truly wanted to host major productions. I can make all the introductions in the world, but if Ireland isn't internationally competitive, it won't matter.

Another problem is the revolving door at the Department of Culture, Heritage and the Gaeltacht. Unfortunately, there is a perception that the department is a political backwater, a portfolio to be endured rather than an opportunity to be embraced. Once, when I told a civil servant that the minister supported something, I was told, "The minister won't be here for long." That's true. In the six-year period of 2007 through 2014, the department had five different ministers. One would have to go back nearly twenty years, to when President Michael D. Higgins was the minister of the department to find a minister in the role who did something with it.

The slow pace means many promising Irish producers, directors, writers, actors, and technicians leave Ireland for places like the US and the UK, where they feel facilitated rather than thwarted. We work to bring many of them together.

In February 2018, *Variety* reported that Pinewood decided to double the size of its complex outside London.

Time will tell the impact of Brexit on the film industry. Had the large studio I'd been advocating been built, and had necessary changes been made, such as doing away with the rule that says a production company cannot be connected to a broadcaster, Ireland could have been well positioned to become the base for major international productions post-Brexit. If a hard border arises between Ireland and the UK, the easy back-and-forth that Star Wars has enjoyed may become more difficult.

Winter Is Coming

During the first year of the Oscar Wilde Awards, I tried to involve what is now called Northern Ireland Screen (NIS), as the event would hold the same networking value for them with their Titanic Paint Hall studio. The first year I approached NIS, I went to their office in Belfast. They said they were interested, but they were getting a new head of marketing, and that person would make those decisions. Then later I was told that they weren't really looking to the US for business. Another year, I was told they had no funds, despite being told previously that money was not an issue. Having tried the civil service route, I eventually contacted the then Democratic Unionist Party (DUP) minister handling the sector, Edwin Poots.

In April 2008, I was in Belfast, where the US-Ireland Alliance was hosting that event marking the tenth anniversary of the Belfast Agreement. While in the city, I asked Minister Poots if he might give me a few minutes of his time. As the DUP had opposed the Northern Ireland peace agreement brokered by Senator Mitchell, no one in the party would be attending our event. Poots agreed, and we met in his office, with his adviser, Paul Givan. Poots had clearly made a few calls prior to my arrival because when I told him I couldn't understand why NIS wasn't supporting something so obviously in its interest, Poots said that NIS staff told him that the LA event was "just a bunch of Irish people talking to Irish people." Given that more than half of our guests were Americans, that was untrue, and so I offered to show Poots the names of many of the Americans who had been at the event. Back at my hotel room, I pulled up the guest list and was able not only to send him a breakdown by nationality but also to give him a list of all the senior executives in the US film business who had attended. Either intentionally or by mistake, I was copied on an email from Poots to the NIS where he showed them what I'd provided and rightly asked, "Why aren't we supporting this?"

During our meeting, Poots told me that he was about to go to Los Angeles to see if he could drum up some film business and said that if I could arrange a few meetings of value to him, he'd see to it that the event was supported. So much for NIS's claim that it wasn't interested in US business. I pulled out all the stops and arranged nearly a dozen high-level meetings for Poots. I heard later that Poots had berated his officials, saying, "Why is it that Vargo can get me a dozen good meetings and the NIS can't get me one?" This, by the way, is another thing that never endears me to civil servants who feel that if we're successful, it makes them look bad in comparison. This constantly hampers many who seek to be helpful to Ireland and Northern Ireland. That attitude is all wrong. The view should be, "Fantastic, she's done all the work for us, used her contacts, helped us get meetings and business." The fault there lies with the manager, Poots in this case, who shouldn't create situations that cause the civil servants to feel threatened by outside assistance.

Poots returned to Northern Ireland happy with what I had arranged, including a meeting with Jimmy Horowitz, the president of Universal Pictures. That began a conversation that ultimately resulted in Universal shooting the film *Your Highness*, starring Danny McBride, James Franco, and Natalie Portman, in Northern Ireland.

When I later followed up with Poots to ask him to make good on his end of the agreement, politics interfered. There was a cabinet reshuffle in Northern Ireland, and Poots was shifted out of the arts and culture portfolio. I had heard through the grapevine that Poots recognized the value of our work and was prepared to override NIS and support the event. Poots was replaced by another DUP member, Gregory Campbell. I knew Campbell from when I worked with Senator Kennedy. In June

2008, I told him of the arrangement with Poots and asked him to fulfill Poots's commitment, "not just because he made the commitment but because you determine as well that it would be of value to Northern Ireland."

I received a reply from Campbell in September 2008, saying that financial constraints meant he couldn't support. Throughout the entire existence of this event, NIS has never contributed to it.

The math is simple. Depending on a variety of factors, the cost of the LA event has been between $150,000 and $250,000 annually. The event is huge value for money. When you consider that *Your Highness* resulted in a nearly $20 million spend in Northern Ireland, it's clear that the event is worth far more than it costs. If Northern Ireland contributed $100,000 a year to our event, it would take two hundred years for them to have contributed as much as was made with the filming of that one movie alone.

Van the Man, Not a Fan

In 2007, we honored Van Morrison at our Oscar Wilde Awards, paying tribute to his music that was used in films.

Like many, I am a fan of Van's music. Before we invited him to be honored, several people in Ireland warned me that I would rue the day.

Shortly after Van agreed to be honored, he started ringing me when I was in Ireland. On more than one occasion, I was summoned to meet him for tea at the Fitzpatrick Castle Hotel in Killiney, just outside of Dublin. Usually, I was a bit perplexed about exactly why he wanted to meet. Perhaps he was just intrigued that I wasn't starstruck and just treated him like I'd treat anyone else.

During one of our conversations, it became clear that Van was very interested in the documentary that Martin Scorsese was making about the Rolling Stones and that he wanted a similar documentary about himself. I said we would be prepared to record his concert at our LA event in high definition and using three cameras, but the deal would have to be that we would both own the video and each of us could use it. Such an undertaking on our part would cost tens of thousands of dollars, and, as a small nonprofit, we wouldn't go down that road without an assurance that we could, at a minimum, recoup our costs. This would also provide him with footage he desired for his documentary.

We had at least two conversations about this, and it was detailed enough that I suggested ways the Alliance might use the footage, such as seeing if Apple or another company that dealt with content for handheld devices might buy the footage. I assured him (it was my suggestion, not something he asked for) that before actually doing anything with the video on my end, I would run the plan by him, as I had no interest in using it in some way that did not do justice to him. Quality and integrity would be at the forefront of any decision. Van agreed.

Months went by, and our team in LA took care of all the elements of recording the concert. Van is an astute businessman and got EMI to release a CD, *Van Morrison at the Movies*, to coincide with our event, and EMI even took out a big ad in the *Los Angeles Times* to congratulate him.

The night before our event, knowing the long day and night before me, I had hoped to go to bed at a reasonable hour. I had an early dinner with friends at the Sunset Marquis, the West Hollywood hotel known for its rock-star clientele. It was also where Van was staying. My early-to-bed plans went by the wayside when I got a call from someone with Van, telling me that he would like to meet me for dinner after the concert he was performing that evening at the Gibson Amphitheatre, a six-thousand-seat theater owned by Universal Studios, which has since been demolished to make way for a Wizarding World of Harry Potter attraction. I had a bad feeling. Why did Van want to see me the night before our event? Wouldn't he be tired after his own concert and either want to see friends or do something other than meet me? Van has a reputation for walking off stage and simply not performing, and I feared the worst. With a few hundred people turning up the next night, including Charlize Theron, Orlando Bloom, and Al Pacino to introduce him, the last thing I wanted was no Van.

I met Van, with a couple of his people, for a late dinner at the Sunset Marquis. Once again, I had no idea why I was summoned. I concluded that he just wanted company while he ate his dinner, as most of the time he wanted to hear me talk about American politics. At some stage, I looked at one of his team with a searching look, as if to ask, *Why am I here?* His assistant just shrugged her shoulders—clearly, she had no idea either. I was just happy that he didn't pull the plug on the concert the next evening.

Earlier that day, Chris Healey, who worked for Van, had emailed me a contract with a note that said he'd bring this contract regarding the filming of the show and that we could sign it at the event the next day, before Van performed. I didn't think much of it at the time, as he wrote in his cover email that it "safeguards both parties."

I believe it was the following morning that I finally had a moment to read the contract. I realized immediately that it actually provided no safeguards for the Alliance. It simply gave Van ownership of the video. While I was concerned, as someone who believes my word is my bond, I assumed this was just some standard way by which Van protected himself and that he would, of course, abide by our agreement that the Alliance too would be able to use the video. It was made very clear to me that if the contract was not signed, Van would not be performing. I called the lawyers on our board and told them about the contract. I noted its contents and that it meant Van owned the video. I felt particularly sandbagged by the fact that Van and I had agreed months ago, and yet no contract was ever suggested or produced earlier; this was sprung on me at the eleventh hour, clearly to have us over a barrel. All the audio and video equipment had been rented, the staff employed, and the venue was already rigged and ready to go; we didn't really have any choice but to sign. I still naively believed that Van, who is a very wealthy man, would have no intention of ripping off a small nonprofit organization. I signed.

Van performed beautifully that night and genuinely seemed to enjoy the evening. SenovvA, the same company that provides video production for the Oscars and production supervision for Elton John's annual Oscar-viewing party, handled the production.

We had only expected Van to sing for fifteen minutes, but he ended up singing for an hour. His daughter, Shana, sang with him, and he involved other guests. Paddy Moloney, founder of the Chieftains, played with him, and Solomon Burke, one of the founders of soul music in the 1960s, joined him in singing "Stand by Me." Maura O'Connell, an old friend and longtime supporter of the Alliance, was in the audience. I'd recalled mentioning to Van how much I liked her cover of his "Crazy Love," and he told me he did as well. I was watching the concert from up in the rafters, and seeing the good mood Van was in, via walkie talkie I had one of our team flag for Van's team that Maura was in the audience. I knew better than to suggest to Van that he should invite anyone to the stage, but I also knew his team would be able to gauge if he would be up for that. They too sensed he was in great form, and a few minutes later, I saw one of his team whisper something to him on stage. Much to Maura's surprise, Van then called her to the stage to sing "Crazy Love" with him. The evening was magical.

Following the performance, as agreed, one HD version of the concert remained with the Alliance; the other was sent to Van. Sometime later, someone in the business of DVD production asked to see the video. After I showed it to him, he told me it was great concert footage that could be made into a DVD and sold. As we wanted to recoup the tens of thousands of dollars we spent on the recording, this seemed to be a proposal worth exploring.

Aware of the contract, as well as my own commitment to Van that I wouldn't do anything without clearing it with him first, I emailed his team to let them know of the offer and that we wished to explore this opportunity.

In September 2007, I received an email from Willie Richardson, identifying himself as Van's manager. He wrote, "I am in negotiations with a number of broadcasters re another Van Morrison project and I am afraid that it would therefore be impossible for the footage to be used in the way you suggest."

I wrote back to him, asking that he raise this with Van directly, given our understanding and given that Mr. Richardson was not present during our conversations in Killiney. Richardson responded to me on October 5, saying that he had discussed this directly with Van and that his previous email was the position.

To say I was annoyed would be an understatement. Again, giving Van the benefit of the doubt, I thought that it could be possible—though doubtful—that others, working on his behalf, had made this decision without ever discussing the matter with him. I then wrote to him directly to make sure there could be no mistake.

I noted in my letter that the US-Ireland Alliance is a small nonprofit organization. We had incurred substantial, additional costs to film the event at the quality I committed to him during our conversations in Killiney. The level of audio, lighting, and video, including recording in HD and with three cameras, was something we did not do previously, nor have we since—we only did so because of his commitment that we would be permitted to recoup our costs.

I said I hoped that he was simply unaware of what transpired since the event, that he was a man of his word, and that he would abide by his commitment. And I noted what I had previously told his team—that if we made any profit above and beyond costs, that money would go to the George J. Mitchell Scholarship program, which allows American students to study in Ireland and Northern Ireland. I had the letter sent by FedEx so there would be certainty that he received it.

Van never replied. I had hoped that, at a minimum, recognizing the costs we incurred, he would at least do the right thing and reimburse us. But no, not even that.

Many in Ireland told me, "We told you so."

The X Factor

At our LA event in 2010, we honored J.J., Seamus McGarvey, and Saoirse Ronan. Tom Cruise attended to present J.J. with his award. Someone told me that Louis Walsh was in town and suggested we invite him. I did not know Walsh personally but knew that he was the manager of Irish boy bands and a judge on Simon Cowell's British talent show, *The X Factor*. So we invited Walsh, who came along on the night.

Melanie Finn wrote a story in Ireland's *Evening Herald* on March 10 about an alleged conversation between Walsh and Tom Cruise at our event. But the story was entirely fictional; Walsh didn't even meet Cruise, much less have a conversation with him.

On the day the story appeared, I was contacted by Cruise's publicist, who had seen it before I did. Understandably, she was wondering where this story came from. Cruise arrived through a back entrance, did his bit, and left immediately after. The entire time he was in the venue, he was with me and his publicist, and Walsh had no conversation with him—a fact that Walsh didn't dispute when I emailed him to ask about the story, which was full of direct quotes from him.

I asked Walsh where the story came from, and I informed Ms. Finn that the conversation simply never happened. Walsh replied that he never spoke to the journalist and claimed he called the paper himself and told them the information was wrong. When I told Finn that Walsh denied speaking with her, she was irate, telling me she was "at a complete loss to understand what your problem is with the story and I fail to see why you continue pursing [sic] this issue." She insisted that she did have a conversation with Walsh, who provided her with the quotes. She told me she had "no idea where you are coming up with this theory that no exchange took place between him and Tom Cruise. As you are not a press representative for Tom Cruise, I fail to see why you have such a greviance [sic] with this story. I am 100 pc confident about my facts of the story." I informed Finn that my problem with the story was that it was fiction (and I knew definitively as I was with Cruise), and Walsh denied speaking with Finn. If she had spoken with Walsh and he had told her the story she wrote, her anger shouldn't have been directed at me, but rather at Walsh, who was denying that he had spoken with her.

Finn then wrote, "I don't see this issue progressing any further this way. I have no idea what your job title is over there or how you claim to know so much about journalism, given that you're not a journalist. Do you have an email you can forward me from Louis Walsh where he says he never had a conversation with a journalist about meeting Tom Cruise at the Oscar Wilde event? Is he denying he ever met Tom Cruise at the event? Also, I am considering forwarding all your emails to the solicitors with Independent Newspapers for impugning my reputation in this manner."

I emailed Finn, Walsh, and the paper's editor, Claire Grady, saying that I had two emails from Walsh denying that he ever spoke to Finn about Tom Cruise. I asked Walsh, whom I copied, that he either give me permission to pass his emails on to Finn, or that he simply clear this up with her directly.

At that point, Walsh and Finn stopped responding. I rang the editor, Claire Grady, and left a message on her voice mail saying that I would like to speak with her about this matter. She did not return my call but sent an email: "Please do not expect a call back from me as I consider it would be completely inappropriate to enter into any discussion with a third party about issues relating to the veracity of stories in the *Herald*. I'm sure that on reflection, you will appreciate that there are no circumstances under which I would discuss with you what Louis Walsh said to our journalist or why he said it."

I was disappointed to learn that an editor did not care at all that the story published in her paper was entirely false. I would have expected that, when I first wrote to Finn, the immediate reaction would have been to want to get to the truth for the sake of her and the paper's reputation. Never once had Finn or Grady expressed concern for the truth.

When Grady refused to retract, I raised the matter with the press ombudsman. The response I received, every step of the way, was that the story didn't do me any personal damage, so I just shouldn't complain. No one cared in the least that the story was completely false.

According to Ireland's Press Council, the Code of Practice states clearly, "In reporting news and information, newspapers and periodicals shall strive at all times for truth and accuracy." It goes on to say that "when a significant inaccuracy, misleading statement or distorted report or picture has been published, it shall be corrected promptly and with due prominence."

As the head of the organization that runs the event, I was not a third party. The matter affects the US-Ireland Alliance and the reputation of Irish journalism. We grew an event to help those in the entertainment field in Ireland interact with their peers in LA. This has resulted in tangible benefits for Ireland. We have had many well-known individuals attend who, in part, are willing to attend because they expect they will be treated fairly. The behavior of Walsh and the *Herald* doesn't help us maintain that reputation.

Dissent. . . . Like medicine, the test of its value is not its taste but its effect, not how it makes people feel at the moment but how it makes them feel and moves them to act in the long run.

—Senator J. William Fulbright

Conclusion

The question I have always had is whether there is sufficient interest in a modern, future-focused relationship between the US and Ireland, when the issues that previously defined it are fading.

It would have never occurred to me, when I founded the US-Ireland Alliance, that anyone who claims to care about the relationship would actively oppose positive contributions to it. But as you have read, they have and do. Is there a critical mass for the positive? The vast majority of Irish Americans aren't that interested in Ireland, and even fewer are involved. Can they become interested?

A Word about the Mitchell Scholarship Program

America's best and brightest are applying for the Mitchell Scholarship to study in Ireland.

British author Martin Walker wrote about Rhodes Scholars in his book, *America Reborn*: "Many of these Rhodes scholars felt only limited affection and nostalgia for Britain as a result of their time at Oxford. . . . They recalled snooty undergraduates, languid dons, cold rooms and bad food." While we recognized the value of a prestigious scholarship in building an informed, nonpartisan constituency knowledgeable about contemporary Ireland, we also recognized that an experience had to be provided that was much more positive. Convinced that, unlike Walker's description of Oxford, a year in Ireland or Northern Ireland can hook the Scholars for a lifetime, we have made every effort to ensure that the Mitchell Scholars return from their year feeling that it has been one of the best of their lives. Judging from their responses, we are achieving that objective.

The Irish universities, and many other organizations and individuals, go out of their way to make sure the Scholars have an interesting year. It is that kind of welcome that is causing students to choose the Mitchell over other opportunities.

Given the nature of politics being about the next election, thinking long-term is a rare enough thing. The US-Ireland Alliance and the Mitchell Scholarship program are about the long game. *Future* leaders are just that, and to see the full value of this program will take decades.

Thinking about who should fund this sort of program brings up interesting issues that can equally be applied to many other worthy causes.

Ireland, Toward a More Equal Relationship

When I sought support from Taoiseach Bertie Ahern in 1998, the scholarship was nothing more than an idea in my head, but he embraced the vision too and took a chance. He knew that the base of Irish influence in Washington was strong but not deep. He knew that those who had always carried the water for Ireland were slowly leaving the stage and that the next generation of America's leaders would need to be educated about the island. His government helped us take our first steps, and within months of our conversation, he announced that the Irish government would contribute the first $3 million toward an endowment to help fund the Mitchell Scholarship program.

Once the Obama administration eliminated our annual funding, the Irish government led by Enda Kenny, and now Leo Varadkar, committed to a number of years of funding. While necessary, it is insufficient to ensure the Mitchell's permanency.

It is our hope that the Irish government will think of the return on investment we've provided. As previously noted, the economic value of Skellig Michael's appearance in *Star Wars* is massive. If the Irish government fully endowed the Mitchell Scholarship program, our high school education plans, and the annual Hollywood event, it still wouldn't come close to that value, and it would ensure that this important Scholarship goes on long after I do.

While I can and do make the case for how this program benefits America, it really is of greatest benefit to Ireland.

Ireland is reaping massive revenue from US companies that have relocated there. In July 2016, the *Sunday Business Post* reported that "since 2008, corporate relocations have boosted Ireland's national income by about €7 billion, according to Department of Finance estimates." That means Ireland gets to collect taxes that aren't being collected in the US. Legal? Yes. But also an argument for why Ireland needs to give back to the relationship. The uncertainty that lies ahead with Brexit is just another reason why Ireland should solidify US ties.

Northern Ireland Has to Give as Well as Take

Aware of the need to build on cross-border initiatives as envisioned by the Mitchell-brokered peace agreement, we felt it important to include Northern Ireland's universities in the program from the outset. In 1998, Mo Mowlam—then Britain's popular secretary of state for Northern Ireland—committed the British government to funding two Scholars every year. When London devolved decision-making to Northern Ireland's Executive, this became a local matter.

During recent budget disputes with London, Northern Ireland's Department of Education and Learning ended its $100,000 annual contribution to the Mitchell Scholarship program. The contribution was minute in the scheme of things, and in exchange, Northern Ireland received America's future leaders, which in turn resulted in a higher profile in the US for Queen's University Belfast and Ulster University. The Marshall is the other prestigious Scholarship that allows Americans to study in Northern Ireland, but a look at recent years of the Marshall program shows that its Scholars are choosing England and Scotland rather than Northern Ireland. The universities in Northern Ireland are great partners, but the government, individuals, and Northern Ireland businesses, including the American companies there, have failed to step up to ensure that America's future leaders have this connection.

Northern Ireland has been counting on London to provide it with a corporate tax rate that allows it to compete with Ireland's 12.5 percent rate. I was always suspicious—would London really annoy Scotland and Wales that way? Regardless, after the Brexit vote, Prime Minister Theresa May pledged to lower the corporate tax to 17 percent by 2020—UK-wide. If that happens, Belfast will look a lot less attractive vis-à-vis London.

England gets future American leaders via the Rhodes and the Marshall. The British government is not inclined to help Northern Ireland compete on this front.

In 2018, when Ireland's Department of Education agreed to provide the Mitchell Scholarship program with three additional years of funding, it did so with the requirement that we bring Queen's University Belfast and Ulster University back into the program and that Ireland would allow its funds to be spent for that purpose. While we're happy to have them back, I'm concerned that Northern Ireland's politicians will be in no hurry to contribute to the program when Ireland is paying their way.

The US Government's Neglect of Europe Has Proved Unwise

The Alliance enjoyed years of bipartisan support for the Mitchell Scholarship program until Secretary of State Hillary Clinton decided to eliminate funding. On the one hand, she rightly complained that too few Americans study abroad but then eliminated already meager funding for scholarships. The Obama administration called for public-private partnerships for funding such things but ignored the fact that the Mitchell achieved that. Furthermore, the administration cared about fostering certain areas of expertise but disregarded the fact that the Mitchell prepares young Americans for leadership positions in such fields.

The Obama administration's pivot to Asia, President Trump's disdain for the State Department and diplomacy, and Trump's disrespect for our traditional allies have led to a weakening of important alliances.

American Companies in Ireland Should Contribute to the Relationship

An EU report in 2016 found that US assets in Ireland equaled €1 trillion. Most American companies with a presence in Ireland have shown relatively little interest in the relationship beyond their ability to avoid paying taxes in the US. Some have a real presence there that predated inversions and tax avoidance strategies, but, for most, this is all about taxes. American companies should be good citizens by contributing to the communities in which they are based, and also to the overall relationship. Given the vast sums that companies like Apple, Microsoft, and others avoid paying in the US by being in Ireland, one would hope they would be a little more visionary about how philanthropy could help solidify ties from which they benefit.

Philanthropists

If you take a look at the people following Bill Gates and Warren Buffett in the pledge to give their fortunes away in their lifetimes, there aren't many Irish surnames on the list. Chuck Feeney is a rare exception. The waning interest of Irish Americans further removed from their ancestral links does not bode well. We remain hopeful that someone would prefer to be remembered for educating our future leaders and tying them to Ireland, rather than for having the most toys when they die.

The Knight-Hennessey Scholars program was recently created to encourage the best and brightest grad students, from around the world, including the US, to go to Stanford. The program has a $750 million endowment from Phil Knight of Nike. Stephen Schwarzman raised $300 million to launch a scholarship for study in China. He made no secret of the fact that he wants that program to compete with the Rhodes. Most people couldn't tell you how Rhodes, Carnegie, or Mellon made their fortunes. They are known today for their philanthropy. We seek a modern-day equivalent.

Postscript

I began writing this book several years ago, and a fairly final draft was finished by the summer of 2016. But I held off on publishing until now because I wanted to give the State Department a reasonable amount of time to address my Freedom of Information request.

That 2010 email Kris Balderston sent to Secretary Clinton (the one that said I "would not succeed" in efforts to obtain funds for the Mitchell Scholarship) was made public at the end of August 2015, and that prompted me to initiate a Freedom of Information request with the department in October 2015.

It has been more than three years since that request was made, and what has been most interesting about an incredibly frustrating process is to "see" what has *not* been provided.

The documents that I did receive are, overwhelmingly, from career foreign service officers or lower-level political appointees. But what I requested were records from high-level political appointees, and I provided the department with a specific list of names.

My name is unusual, so records should not be that difficult to find.

This raises questions. Were State Department officials, in addition to Secretary Clinton, communicating outside the official State Department system? Were records that were created inside the system destroyed? I have several emails from a couple of the individuals on the list I provided the State. At a minimum, the department should have found these emails in its own search for records.

I wrote this book for the same reason I created the US-Ireland Alliance, in hopes of finding others who might be interested in a modern reimagining of a historic relationship. As this book has shown, there are several people who profess to care about the relationship but whose actions suggest otherwise. I hope that there is interest and that the positive will prevail.

Acknowledgments

When I started the US-Ireland Alliance in 1998, with nothing more than an idea in my head, a few people not only jumped early but have remained with me throughout two decades. There aren't words to adequately express my gratitude to Brian Barrington, Mark Nagel, Gerry McCrory, Jim Fitzpatrick, and Eric Lieberman.

Many thanks to those who read drafts of this book, parts of it, or just gave me helpful advice along the way: Paul Tweed, Bill Shipsey, Lisa E. Davis, Melissa Georges, Brian Barrington, Mark Nagel, Joe O'Malley, Conor Ryan, Paul Feldstein, Mary Lou Hartman, Cliff Sloan, Gerry McCrory, Garrett Kelleher, Ruth Shipsey, Ellen Bork, Kathleen Barrington, Mary Calpin, Paul Hayes, Victoria Kelly, and John and Noelle Pierce.

Thank you to C. S. Farrelly, Cavan Bridge Press, everyone at Girl Friday Productions, and YJ Heo.

While this book considers the problems in the relationship, there are so many people who have allowed the US-Ireland Alliance to be successful for now twenty years:

The late senator Ted Kennedy and Carey Parker, generous mentors who encouraged me to follow my vision and take the leap. Senator George J. Mitchell who graciously permitted me to name our scholarship after him, and for the time he has given to the Scholars. who share his commitment to service.

Bernie and John Gallagher, Michael Smurfit, the late Donal Geaney, and Brendan Hickey—they all jumped early with me. Former taoiseach Bertie Ahern and the late secretary of state for Northern Ireland, Mo Mowlam, for seeing the possibilities, and for not needing reports or conferences to do so.

Derek and Siobhan Quinlan, Garrett and Maeve Kelleher, Bernard and Moira McNamara, Chuck Feeney, Sean O'Sullivan, several members of Congress and of the Oireachtas, and some who wish to remain anonymous. And to the Irish and Northern Ireland universities, great partners in this venture.

I am grateful to those who have been on the staff of the US-Ireland Alliance over the years, with special thanks to Mitchell Scholarship directors Dell Pendergrast, Mary Lou Hartman, Serena Wilson, and Carolina Chavez—for their unique contributions and for remaining connected to the Scholars and the program.

Katie McGrath and J.J. Abrams for sharing Bad Robot—not to mention for putting a certain Jedi on Skellig Michael. Deirdre and Buzz O'Neill, Richard Mooney, Lindsay McConchie, Kevin Harvey, Ted Kroeber, and the team at Bad Robot—sanity in a sea of insanity. Everyone who is part of our Cultúr Club, and those who have supported it. The many artists who have been a part of the Oscar Wilde Awards—I am in awe of your creativity and thankful for your generosity.

All of those who have served on our selection committees and those who make certain the Scholars have a great year in Ireland. For the Mitchell Scholars—you inspire me.

Thanks to everyone at Hayes Solicitors, Arnold & Porter, and Skadden Arps.

The Doyle Collection for lovely homes away from home.

Mark Patrick Hederman, Nóirín Ní Riain, the monks at Glenstal Abbey, Laurence Crowley, Una Fox, Hylda Queally,

Jim Sheridan, the late Sir George Quigley, Joanne McGrath, John O'Donoghue, Dom Bryan, Pete Shirlow, Dearbhla Molloy, Dermot Crowley, Sean MacCartaigh, Chris Armstrong, Felimy Greene, Tom McEnery, Ruairi Quinn, Liz O'Donnell, Monica McWilliams, Geraldine McAteer, Tom Byrne, and several Irish ambassadors—particularly Rory Montgomery, Sean O hUiginn, Noel Fahey, Dan Mulhall, Adrian O'Neill, and Eamonn McKee. Thanks also to Norman Houston at the Northern Ireland Bureau.

Space does not permit me to list all the donors, supporters, and members of the various boards of the Alliance, of the Mitchell Scholarship program, and of our Oscar Wilde Awards, but they may be found on the US-Ireland Alliance website at www.us-irelandalliance.org.

Apologies to those I've surely missed here.

Most important, to my family and friends—here and gone—I am grateful for your love and support.

About the Author

Trina Vargo is the president of the US-Ireland Alliance, an organization she founded in 1998. From late 1987 until April 1998, she was employed by Senator Edward M. Kennedy and served as his foreign policy adviser during the critical years of the Northern Ireland peace process.

Vargo created the US-Ireland Alliance to build ties between the US and the island of Ireland for future generations. She also created the George J. Mitchell Scholarship program, which sends future American leaders to institutions of higher learning on the island of Ireland for a year of graduate study. More than three hundred Americans apply annually for one of the twelve prestigious Scholarships. There are now more than two hundred Mitchell Scholars. Vargo created the annual Oscar Wilde Awards to honor the Irish in entertainment. The annual event is currently held at J.J. Abrams's Bad Robot production company in Santa Monica. Vargo has played an important role in encouraging film production in Ireland, including the filming of *Star Wars: The Force Awakens.*

Working directly with political leaders in Northern Ireland, the Clinton administration, and the Irish government, Vargo served as a key behind-the-scenes player in the Northern Ireland peace process, aiding in the granting of a visa for Sinn Fein leader Gerry Adams to visit the US in 1994. That visa was central to the subsequent IRA cease-fire and the peace talks that led to the 1998 Belfast Agreement. As a foreign policy adviser to Kennedy, Vargo had a wide-ranging portfolio that included imposing sanctions on Libya following the 1988 bombing of Pan Am Flight 103; spearheading the efforts to bring free and fair elections to Guyana in 1992; changing the way the State Department analyzed United Nations voting patterns, which impacted foreign aid eligibility; and getting Jews out of the former Soviet Union and Syria, and Americans out of China after Tiananmen Square.

Vargo also served as the adviser on Irish issues to the campaigns of every Democratic nominee for president from Michael Dukakis through Barack Obama. She advised several American ambassadors to Ireland going back to the mid-1990s when Jean Kennedy Smith was nominated as President Clinton's ambassador. She also served as an adviser to Madeleine Albright when she was preparing for her Senate confirmation hearings to become the US ambassador to the UN. Vargo has addressed the Joint Committee on Foreign Affairs in the Oireachtas (the Irish Parliament).

With the achievement of the Northern Ireland peace agreement and the massive economic advancement of Ireland in the 1990s, Vargo recognized how the relationship between the US and the island of Ireland would naturally change, something she first wrote about in the *Washington Post* on the launch of the US-Ireland Alliance in 1998.

The Alliance has held golf tournaments in Ireland to introduce leading American executives to their Irish counterparts, which has resulted in business for both countries. The Alliance also provides materials for high school teachers to teach about Ireland.

In 2007, Vargo wrote a prescient piece on immigration reform as it pertained to the Irish. While it made her the bête noire of a small number of vocal individuals, her article was broadly welcomed, including by the former Irish prime minister Garrett Fitzgerald, politicians, business leaders, emigration experts, and immigration leaders. A few months after her piece appeared in the *Irish Times*, Irish prime minister Bertie Ahern articulated similar views when he visited the United States.

Born and raised in central Pennsylvania, Vargo graduated from the University of Pittsburgh with degrees in political science and history. As the recipient of a Rotary International Scholarship, she attended McGill University in Montreal, where she obtained an MA degree in political science with a concentration in international relations.

Made in the USA
Lexington, KY
19 July 2019